AF484456

Yoruba Mythology

Captivating Myths and Legends of the Yoruba and Other West African Peoples

Free Bonus from Captivating History (Available for a Limited time)

Hi History Lovers!

Now you have a chance to join our exclusive history list so you can get your first history ebook for free as well as discounts and a potential to get more history books for free! Simply visit the link below to join.

Captivatinghistory.com/ebook

Also, make sure to follow us on Facebook, Twitter and Youtube by searching for Captivating History.

Table of Contents

Introduction

This collection of stories brings together tales from across West Africa, from the Yoruba and Hausa of Nigeria to the Mandinka and Soninke of Mali to the Jabo of Liberia and more. Each culture represented in this volume has its own rich storytelling tradition, one that carries on today in Africa and within the African Diaspora in the Caribbean and the United States.

Some of these stories are built on tropes that can be found the world over, such as the so-called "Cinderella story" or the tale of the wise commoner who outwits the king. Other stories are particular to West African culture and history, portraying the deeds of important historical figures—albeit often fictionalized, or emphasizing the power of stories and storytelling in West African culture.

The first part of this book contains stories of kings and heroes. Each of these stories presents a different examination of the meaning of power and what consequences may follow from the use or misuse of that power.

The courage and cleverness of women are the subjects of the second part of the book, which contains stories of queens and young girls saving themselves, their families, or their countries from destruction. Some of these stories involve women outwitting the villains, while others involve using strength or kindness to overcome opposition. All of them involve magic in one way or another and perseverance on the part of the heroines.

The spirit world and its interactions with humans are the subjects of part three. In some cases, the spirits work to teach the humans a lesson, sometimes through the law of unintended consequences, but in others, the humans work to free themselves from the oppression of spirits and monsters who are holding them captive in some way.

The final part of this book contains stories of punishment and reward. The characters in these tales find themselves on fortune's wheel, gaining things that are good and losing them again. These stories explore what it means to gain things and lose them again and the consequences that both gain and loss can sometimes bring.

Many collections of stories from Africa focus on animal tales, and not without reason, since the corpus of African animal tales is both rich and varied. This volume instead concentrates on stories about human actors trying to make their way through a complicated world. This world includes animals and many supernatural forces, but the main characters are themselves humans struggling with the obstacles that life has put in their path. Thus, these stories explore ideas about strength and weakness, wisdom and folly, gain and loss, desire and power, and all the other things that make us human.

Part I: Kings and Heroes

The Staff of Oranyan (*Yoruba, Nigeria*)

Oranyan was a historical king from the city of Ilé-Ifè who established the city of Oyo-Ifè. Oyo-Ifè became the capital of the Oyo Empire, which existed in parts of what is now Benin City and Western Nigeria, beginning in the late twelfth century and continuing until the colonization of Nigeria by the British in the late nineteenth century. The historical Oranyan was known as a formidable warrior and hunter, and an obelisk known as the Staff of Oranyan still can be seen today in the city of Ilé-Ifè. This story partly explains how the Staff of Oranyan came to be erected.

Oranyan's descendants still retain a royal title and play important roles in Nigerian politics. The late Lamidi Olayiwola Adeyemi III (1938–2022), the Alaafin, or traditional ruler, of the city of Oyo, founded an annual festival in his ancestor Oranyan's honor in 2012.

Long, long ago, when the world was new, there was a king named Oranyan. Oranyan was a just ruler and fiercely defended his kingdom of Ilé-Ifè. Under Oranyan's rule, Ilé-Ifè became a large and prosperous place, and this prosperity was a temptation to kings from other places who wished to have Ilé-Ifè for their own. Whenever kings from other places brought their armies to Ilé-Ifè to fight, Oranyan did not stay at home and conduct affairs from the safety of his palace; he led his army into battle. Oranyan fought alongside his soldiers, his sharp sword cutting its way through swaths of enemies. Soon, other kings learned there was no point in assailing Ilé-Ifè; Oranyan's armies were too powerful, and Oranyan was worth a whole army by himself.

After Oranyan had ruled for many long years, there came a time that he felt his life would soon be over.

He summoned all his subjects to the marketplace and said, "My people, it is time for me to leave this world. I ask you to have courage and defend our beloved Ilé-Ifè just as I would if I were still with you. But never fear—should mortal peril threaten our city, I will come back to defend you. I will teach the old men the proper words to say and things to do, and they will be able to bring me back."

The people wept, for Oranyan was a beloved leader, and they didn't want to see him go.

"What will we do without you?" they cried. "Please, stay with us forever."

"I cannot stay. Have courage. I will return when you need me. I have promised."

Oranyan taught the secret words to the elders among the people. Then he strode out into the center of the marketplace and thrust the end of his staff into the ground, where it turned into a column of stone.

"Here, I have planted my staff," Oranyan said. "I have planted it here to remind you that you are the people of Ilé-Ifè, who have nothing to fear, and I will always return to help you."

When news of Oranyan's death reached the ears of a nearby king, he thought to himself, *Oho, Oranyan is dead! Let's see whether Ilé-Ifè can stand before me now!*

And so he mustered his army and descended upon Ilé-Ifè, thinking it would be easy to take the city now that Oranyan was gone. At first, the battle went badly against the army of Ilé-Ifè, and the people began to fear that they would be conquered.

The people went to the elders and said, "Call back Oranyan! He said to call upon him if we were ever in mortal peril, and surely that time is now!"

The elders heartily agreed, so they went into the marketplace and said the secret words, calling upon Oranyan. No sooner had they finished speaking than the ground began to shake. There was a noise like a thunderclap, and a great fissure opened in the ground at the elders' feet. Out of the fissure came Oranyan, grasping his sword and dressed for battle. Oranyan ran out to the battlefield, where he saw the soldiers of Ilé-Ifè being worsted. Oranyan leaped into the fray, slashing to one side and then to the other with his mighty sword until the tide of battle was turned and the enemies were routed. Oranyan and the soldiers of Ilé-Ifè pursued the fleeing warriors and killed every last one of them.

The warriors returned to Ilé-Ifè, where the people met them with much rejoicing, everyone thanking Oranyan for honoring his promise. Oranyan, for his part, said nothing but stamped on the ground in the marketplace, whereupon a fissure opened up. Oranyan went into the fissure and descended into the earth. The ground closed over his head, and the marketplace looked like nothing had ever happened there.

Other kings soon heard what had happened at Ilé-Ifè, that the army of one of their brother kings had been completely annihilated, and Oranyan himself had come back from the dead to fight on behalf of his people.

"It is impossible to win a war with a ghost," the other kings said. "Especially a ghost as strong and skilled as Oranyan. We will leave Ilé-Ifè alone."

Many years passed, and Ilé-Ifè became even more prosperous, but no outside king dared to send so much as a scouting party to molest it. One day, there was a great festival in Ilé-Ifè. The people played drums, sang, and danced. They ate good food and drank great quantities of palm wine.

No one knows who first had the idea, but soon people were saying, "Old Oranyan has been away for a very long time. It's not really fair that he should only have to come to visit when there's danger. We should invite him to the festival! He should come and celebrate with us!"

A group of people then went to the elders and asked them to summon Oranyan.

"Oranyan deserves to have some fun," they said. "Bring him back so he can sing and dance and drink with us!"

The elders were shocked by this request. "Summoning Oranyan is only to happen when the city is in peril. Oranyan himself said so. We will not summon him for such a frivolous reason. Go back to the festival and stop thinking such foolish thoughts."

"Oh, come on," the people replied. "Don't be such sticks-in-the-mud. Think of poor old Oranyan, sitting there with nothing to do, no palm wine to drink, and no one to dance with. Summon him now!"

The elders resisted, but finally, they saw it would be no use. They went into the marketplace and used the secret words to summon Oranyan. As before, a fissure opened up in the earth, and out came Oranyan, ready for battle. Now, it was late at night, and many people in the marketplace were making a great deal of noise. Oranyan believed the enemies had managed to enter the city itself and were swarming through the marketplace, so he began to strike out with his sword. People began to scream and run for their lives, but Oranyan hunted every last one of them down, thinking them to be enemies. It wasn't until dawn finally broke that Oranyan saw that he had slain his own people.

Oranyan dropped his sword and fell to his knees in grief.

"Why did you summon me?" he cried. "Why did you tell me the city was in peril when there were only my own people here in the streets? I will never fight again. Never again will you be able to summon me. I will stay away forever."

Then Oranyan stamped on the ground so that the fissure opened up again. He went down into the earth, and the earth closed over his head, and from that day forward, he was never seen. The only thing that remains of him is his staff of stone, which still stands in the marketplace even today.

Bayajidda (*Hausa, Nigeria*)

This story is the foundation legend for the ancient Hausa state of Daura, located in what is now Katsina Province in the arid Sahel region of Northern Nigeria. According to the legend, Bayajidda came to West Africa from Baghdad and, upon his arrival, performed deeds that led him to become the first king of Daura. One of these deeds was the slaying of a snake that had been preventing people from getting water from a well called the Kusugu Well. The Kusugu Well still exists today and is available for tourists to visit.

Bayajidda's story is preserved in a collection of writings in Arabic known as the Girgam. *The* Girgam *chronicles the history of the Kanem-Bornu Empire, which existed in Eastern West Africa between the eighth century and the middle of the nineteenth century.*

Once there was a man named Bayajidda, who was the son of the king of Baghdad. Bayajidda quarreled with his father and was in ill favor with the people of the city, so he decided to leave, taking with him a portion of Baghdad's armies and the soldiers' families. Bayajidda and his people traveled westward until they came to Bornu, where they made their home. The king of Bornu saw them settling there, and he was afraid because he saw that Bayajidda's army was mightier than his.

"What should I do about these newcomers and their leader?" the king asked his counselors.

"If you want him to be an ally rather than an enemy, give him one of your daughters in marriage," the counselors replied.

And so it was that the king of Bornu went to Bayajidda, giving to him in marriage his daughter, Magira. In this way, the king of Bornu made an alliance with Bayajidda.

Sometime later, the king of Bornu went to Bayajidda and said, "I need to make war on my enemies. Will you lend me some of your soldiers and horsemen? Whichever of them returns from the battle with me will be richly rewarded."

"Certainly, you may take some of my men," Bayajidda replied and commanded three thousand of his soldiers and horsemen to go with the king of Bornu to fight.

The king of Bornu was on a campaign for six months, and although he had married his daughter to Bayajidda and accepted soldiers and horsemen from him, he still feared the young Baghdadi prince. He was always thinking of ways he could get rid of him. When the king of Bornu returned from the campaign, he again met with his counselors to discuss what might be done with Bayajidda. Magira overheard their conversation and ran back home to tell her husband.

"My father is plotting to kill you," Magira said. "And taking soldiers and horsemen from you was a way to weaken you. He always planned to keep them after doing away with you."

Bayajidda then called together all the people who had journeyed with him from Baghdad.

"We cannot stay here," he said. "The king of Bornu has only pretended to be a friend. He intends to kill me, and I fear for your safety if you stay. Gather up your belongings and ride north. Hopefully, you will find a safe place to live."

"But where will you go?" the people asked.

"I am a danger to you if I stay. I will go elsewhere, and it's best you don't know where."

The people did as Bayajidda commanded. They gathered up their belongings and rode north. Bayajidda himself rode westward with his wife, Magira, and concubine. At this time, Magira was pregnant, and when they stopped to rest in a place called Gabas ta Buram, she was stricken with her pains and bore a son. Magira was not ready to travel onward, so Bayajidda left her there in Gabas ta Buram and rode on with his concubine, who was also with child.

Bayajidda and his concubine continued westward until they came to the city of Daura. When they arrived, night had already fallen. The journey had been long, and Bayajidda and his concubine were thirsty, so they knocked on the door of a nearby house.

When an old woman answered the door, Bayajidda said, "Greetings, Mother. My concubine and I have traveled a long way and are thirsty. Have you any water to give us?"

"If I had any I would surely share it with you," the old woman replied, whose name was Waira. "But water can only be got in Daura on Fridays, and today is not Friday."

"What prevents you?" Bayajidda asked.

"A great serpent lives at the bottom of the well, and it bites anyone who tries to take water, except on Fridays. The snake's name is Sarki, and its bite is venomous, so once bitten, a person dies soon thereafter. No one here dares to go for water except on Fridays."

"Give me your bucket, Mother, and tell me how to get to this well. I will see to the serpent."

Waira handed her bucket to Bayajidda and gave him directions to the well. Bayajidda soon arrived at the well and lowered his bucket into it. No sooner had the bucket touched the water than a giant serpent shot out of the well, mouth agape, fangs gleaming in the moonlight. Bayajidda took his sword and swept the great snake's head from its body with one stroke. He drew water, picked up the head, and brought it back to Waira's house, leaving the snake's headless body beside the well.

"Here is the head of the snake, Mother, and a bucket full of water. Now, you and your fellow citizens may have water any time you need it," Bayajidda said.

Waira then invited Bayajidda and his concubine to be her guests, thanking Bayajidda for his deed.

In the morning, people gathered around the well to view the serpent's body. Everyone wondered who had slain the snake, and finally, a messenger was sent to Queen Daura to tell her that the city had been rid of the scourge of the serpent. She immediately mounted her horse and went with the princes of her realm to see for herself that the story was true. When she arrived, the crowd parted to let her through, and she saw that the great serpent had indeed been killed.

"Who has done this deed?" the queen asked. "He shall be richly rewarded with half of my city."

"I slew the snake!" several voices shouted at once.

"Show me the head, if you speak true," the queen said, but the people had to admit that they were not the ones who had slain the snake, and after that, no one else dared claim that deed.

"I know who killed the snake," Waira said, who had gone down to the well in the morning with the other townsfolk. "He is a guest in my house. He arrived last night with his concubine and asked for water. When I explained about the snake, he took my bucket and came to the well. He returned to my house with a bucket full of water and the head of the snake."

The queen then sent messengers to Waira's house, commanding Bayajidda to come to the well with the snake's head.

Bayajidda did so, and the queen said, "You have done my people a great service. Your reward is to have half of my city."

"I thank your majesty—that is very generous. But I would rather have your hand in marriage, if you consent."

"I consent," the queen replied.

And so, Bayajidda married Queen Daura and moved into her palace with his concubine. There Bayajidda ruled along with the queen, who entrusted him with meeting all embassies and messengers who came to her palace.

In time, Bayajidda's concubine gave birth to her child, a son who she named Mukarbigari. The queen also had a son by Bayajidda, and this son was named Bawogari. When Bayajidda died, his son Bawo became king. Bawo's six sons later became kings themselves, the rulers of six of the seven original Hausa states, the *Hausa Bokoi.*

The King Who Sought Poverty (*Benin*)

This parable from Benin aptly describes the dehumanization that can accompany poverty. It also underlines the ignorance that privilege can convey to the wealthy, for if the king had known what poverty meant, he never would have tried to find it for himself.

Once there was a king of Adja. His name was Adjahosu, and he was a very wealthy man. He had more food than he could eat. He had more clothes than he could wear. He had more money than he could spend. However, one thing he did not have: The knowledge about what it was like to be poor.

One day, Adjahosu went to his diviner and said, "I am a very wealthy man. I know what it's like to have everything, but I want to know what it is like to be poor. Tell me what I must do to gain this knowledge."

The diviner consulted his tools, and when he was satisfied he had the answer, he replied, "Tell your hunters to go into the bush and capture a giraffe. They must bring the giraffe back alive. While the hunters are gone, you need to get a drum, a gong, some rattles, and a long strip of cloth. I'll tell you what to do with those when the hunters come back."

The king did as the diviner bid him. He told his hunters to capture a giraffe and bring it back alive, and he went and collected the things the diviner told him to collect.

When the hunters arrived with the giraffe, the diviner said to the hunters, "Tie the drum, gong, and rattles around the giraffe's neck."

When this was done, the diviner said to the king, "Get onto the giraffe's back."

When the king was astride the giraffe, the diviner said to the hunters, "Now tie him in place with the cloth."

When that was done, the diviner handed a stick to the king and said, "Strike the drum with this."

No sooner had the king struck the drum than the giraffe bolted into the bush, the king struggling to cling to the animal's back. The faster the giraffe ran, the more noise the rattles and gong made. The more noise the rattles and gong made, the more frightened the giraffe became. The giraffe ran across plains and through forests, finally running through a thicket of thorn bushes whose long, sharp thorns tore through the cloth that bound the king to the giraffe's back. The king fell to the ground, utterly bewildered and frightened. He had no idea where he was. He had no idea what route the giraffe had taken because he was too busy holding on to take note of his surroundings, so he had no idea how to get home, and now the sun was setting. The king looked around him in despair. There were no signs of any village or caravan or encampment of hunters anywhere, no sign of anyone who could help him or give him a safe place to sleep.

In the end, the king climbed a tree and slept there, hoping he would not fall down or be discovered by a passing leopard. The next day, the king set about trying to find food and water. Sometimes, he was successful; sometimes, he was not, and he went to sleep both hungry and thirsty. The king lived like this for three months, at one point losing one of his eyes.

The first human being the king saw in those three months was a gnarled old woman who had come into the bush looking for indigo plants.

The king went up to her and said, "Oh, thank the gods you're here. Can you tell me the way to the nearest village?"

The woman did not recognize the king. She had never so much as seen a picture of him before, so she had no idea that it was King Adjahosu who stood before her, nor that he was even a royal person at all, for he was very dirty, blind in one eye, dressed in ragged clothing, and clearly had not been eating well. The old woman took pity on the poor king.

"Come with me," she said and led him to her home.

When the woman and the king arrived at her home, she gave him food and clean clothing, and water to bathe in. The woman was a dyer, so once a week, she would go to the market to buy cloth to dye. When the cloth was dyed and ready to sell, Adjahosu carried it to market for her. The woman and Adjahosu lived and worked together in this way for three years.

Now, Adjahosu's family had no idea where the king had gone. No one had been able to follow the trail of the giraffe, and no one had arrived with a message saying where Adjuhosu was. There came a day when one of the king's sons desired to have some dyed cloth, so he sent a messenger to the old woman asking her to meet him in a certain field. The woman came as she was commanded, and Adjuhosu came with her to carry the dyed cloth. When they arrived at the field, they found two of the king's sons waiting for them. The king's sons looked closely at the man with the old woman, and they wondered whether this might be their father, for although he only had one eye, he greatly resembled Adjuhosu. Adjuhosu, for his part, did not recognize his sons.

The sons finished purchasing the cloth, and just as they were leaving, they heard the old woman say, "Adjuhosu, now we will sell some wood. Go and fetch some to sell," and the man went into the bush to collect wood.

Their business concluded, the king's sons went home. Immediately they went to their eldest brother and said, "The strangest thing happened today. When we met that old dyer to buy some cloth, she had a manservant named Adjuhosu with her. The man had only one eye but looked a lot like our father. Then the dyer told the manservant to fetch wood to sell, and the manservant went. If he looks like our father and has our father's name, could this perhaps be our father?"

"Perhaps it is," the eldest brother replied. "I will go to the next market and find out for sure."

On the next market day, the eldest brother went to the market and waited for the old woman. She soon arrived, her manservant carrying a bundle of dyed cloth on his head. The man put down the cloth and took his machete to go and cut some wood in the bush. After a little while, he returned with a bundle of wood, which he set down next to the cloth, and then the woman gave him a bowl of food. The man took the food a little way away from the woman and sat down to eat.

The son was sure this was his father.

The son went up to the manservant and said, "Father?"

When Adjuhosu looked up, he saw his eldest son standing there. Adjuhosu leaped to his feet and embraced his son. Father and son held one another and wept for joy.

The son then took his father to the old woman and said, "Where did you find this man?"

"I was out looking for indigo in the bush and found him there," the old woman replied.

"Sell him to me."

"I can't do that! I need a servant to carry things for me. How else will I sell my goods at market?"

"I will pay you enough that you can buy another servant to help you."

"I don't want another servant. This one works hard. Another one might not work as hard. And what's he to you, anyway?"

"He is my father."

"Oh, well, if he is your father, then he should go with you."

And so, Adjuhosu went back to the palace with his son and was reunited with his family. Adjuhosu's son gave him fresh clothing and fresh water to bathe in. Sometime later, Adjuhosu assembled all his family to hear his story. He told them about being lost in the bush and his years of servitude with the old woman.

"I did those things because I wanted to know what it was like to be poor," Adjuhosu said. "And now I know. Poverty is hunger and thirst. In poverty, you have nothing of your own. Never wish for poverty."

Gassire's Lute (*Soninke, Mali and other West African countries*)

This myth of the Soninke people captures the importance both of the Dausi, a collection of oral epics that date back to the fourth century A.D., and also of Wagadu, which is both the name of a city and the Ghana Empire, which existed between c. 300 and c. 1100 A.D. in what are now parts of Mauritania and Mali. The Dausi was originally performed by wandering bards, and although these oral epics are still performed as such today, they were not set down in writing until fairly late. The arrival of Islam in West Africa in the eighth century also corroded the Dausi tradition since many of the stories incorporated into the Dausi ceased to be told after the population left their old ways behind in favor of the new religion. "Gassire's Lute," retold below, is one of the Dausi stories that has survived to the present day.

Long, long ago, there was a great empire called Wagadu. Wagadu rose and fell four times, and each time, it had a different name. The first name of Wagadu was Dierra, and it is in Dierra that this story happened, the story of the great hero, Gassire, and his lute.

The King of Dierra was Nganamba Fasa. He was a great king who ruled well. He was a valiant warrior who fought like a lion, and every time he led the Fasa army into battle against the Boroma and the Burdama, he returned victorious. However, Nganamba was growing old. He was so old that his son, Gassire, was a man with eight sons, all grown to manhood themselves.

Gassire desperately wanted to be king. He wanted to be the one to rule, to lead the army into battle bearing the king's shield and the king's sword, but Nganamba continued living and ruling, so Gassire could not have his desire. Like his father, Gassire was a great warrior. Every time he led his troops into battle, he returned victorious. Gassire lived for the thrill of battle and the fame of the hero.

Yet, no matter how victorious or famous he became, it was never enough because in his heart, he wondered, *When will Nganamba die? When will I get to be king?*

One night, when Gassire lay in his bed yearning for the day when he would be king, he decided that he could no longer stand the waiting and yearning. He went to the house of a wise old man named Kiekorro and knocked on the door.

"Who is there?" Kiekorro asked.

"It is I, Gassire."

Kiekorro let Gassire in. "What brings you here at this hour of the night?"

"I have a question in my heart that can wait no longer. I need to know when my father will die. I need to know when I will be king in Dierra and carry the sword and shield of the king."

"Your father will indeed die someday, but you will not rule. You will not carry the sword and shield of the king. You will be a bard, and you will carry a lute, and because of this, Wagadu will fall."

Gassire was aghast. "I came to you because everyone says you are wise, but I see that you are nothing but a teller of tales. Wagadu is strong! Our warriors win every battle they fight!"

"I know you don't believe me, but one day, you will. This will happen on the day when you are in the field and hear the partridges sing, and you will understand their song. By that song, you will know your path and the path that Wagadu must also follow."

The next day, there was to be a great battle between the army of Wagadu and the Burdama.

Gassire led his men to the plain where the battle was to be fought, but when they were about to array themselves for battle, Gassire said, "You don't need to fight today. I will fight the Burdama by myself."

Gassire said this because he was so full of anger over what Kiekorro had told him the night before that he thought his heart might burst if he did not do some valorous deed beyond anything he had ever done.

And so it was that Gassire rode out and fought the Burdama alone. He rode up on his white charger and lay about him with his sword with such strength and skill that no man could stand against him. He mowed down the Burdama warriors as a farmer mows down grain with his scythe at the time of harvest.

Soon, the Burdama warriors were saying, "This is no man! This is a spirit of some kind! We cannot stand against him!"

Hence, they threw down their spears and ran away.

Gassire ordered his warriors to gather all the Burdama spears and bring them back to the city in triumph. All the way back, the warriors sang the praises of Gassire, for never had they seen any hero fight so fiercely, and never had they won as many spears in one battle as they had today.

That evening, Gassire bathed and dressed in clean clothing, but instead of joining his warriors at the feast celebrating their victory, he wandered out of the city and into the fields. In the fields, he heard partridges singing in the bushes. Gassire listened and found that he could understand what the birds were singing.

One of them sang, "This is my Dausi! This is the song of my deeds! Kings die, heroes die, and empires fall. I myself will die because all creatures that live upon the earth must die. But my Dausi will never die! The song of my deeds will live on, even after kings and heroes have all turned to dust! The song of my deeds will live on, even after empires are no more!"

As soon as Gassire heard this, he ran to the wise old man's house.

"Keikorro!" he said. "Kiekorro, I heard the partridges in the field, and I understood their songs, just as you told me would happen. One partridge sang his Dausi and said it would live on long after he was gone. Tell me, wise one, do men also sing the Dausi? Do the Dausi cheat death? Do they really last longer than kings or empires?"

"Now maybe you will understand why I said you are to be a bard, not a king. Let me tell you about the Dausi. When the Fasa people lived near the coast, they had enemies who sang the Dausi, and these Dausi were fearsome to hear. The Fasa themselves did not sing the Dausi because people of their rank, the people of the Horro, did not sing them. That duty was for the people of the next rank below them, the people of the Diare. The Horro and Diare fought in battle together, and many heroes came from each. Maybe since you cannot be the highest one of the Horro, you should be the highest one of Diare. But Wagadu will still fall because of it."

"Wagadu can do what it likes. I care not."

The next day, Gassire went to a man who made instruments of music and asked him to make a lute.

"I can make you a lute," the man replied. "But it will not sing for you."

"I will make it sing," Gassire said. "Just make it for me, and you'll see."

The man made a fine lute for Gassire and gave it to him. Gassire plucked and strummed at the strings; however, the lute did not make a sound.

Gassire returned it to the man who had made it and said, "This lute won't sing."

"Yes, I told you it wouldn't," the man replied.

"Can't you fix it?"

"No, only you can do what must be done to make it sing."

"What must I do?"

"This lute is only a thing made of wood. Things made of wood have no hearts. Only things with a heart can sing, so you must give this lute a heart. You must carry the lute into battle with you. The lute must hear the ring of your sword. The lute must be wetted with the blood of your blood and breath of your breath. The lute must absorb your pain. The lute must absorb your fame. Only then will the lute have a heart of its own. Only when your sons die and shed their blood onto your lute will it have a voice, and your sons shall live on in the voice of the lute. But Wagadu will still be lost even so."

"Wagadu can do what it likes. I care not."

The next day, Gassire told his sons that they were going to do battle with the Burdama.

"This will not be any ordinary battle," he said. "The Dausi of this battle shall live forever. Our names shall live forever in the Dausi."

Then Gassire told his younger sons to stay behind and that only the eldest was to fight that day. And fight he did: Gassire and his son rode into the ranks of the Burdama, where they fought not like men but powerful spirits, and none could stand before them.

At one point, Gassire was surrounded by eight Burdama warriors. Gassire's son came to his father's aid, slaying four of the Burdama; however, a Burdama warrior thrust out his spear, piercing Gassire's son's heart. Gassire fell into a rage that his son had been killed, and such was his rage that the Burdama took fright and fled. Gassire picked up his son's body and draped it over his shoulder, where the blood dripped onto the lute that Gassire carried on his back. In this way, Gassire led his warriors back to Diera, and all the city mourned the death of Gassire's son.

In the evening, after his son's funeral, Gassire took his lute and strummed and plucked the strings, but still, they would not sing for him. Gassire again flew into a rage. Again, he told his sons they would go out to fight the Burdama in the morning. Again, he had only one of his sons fight alongside him, and again, his son was killed. Again, Gassire brought his son's body home over his shoulder and the blood dripped onto the lute; however, still the lute would not sing.

For five more days, Gassire did the same thing. He led his warriors into battle with the Burdama, and at the end, he brought home the body of one of his sons, the blood dripping into the lute.

The people were constantly in mourning for Gassire's sons and the others who had died in battle.

On the eve of the eighth day, the men of Dierra went to Gassire and said, "Enough. We are all brave men, and you know this, so you will listen to us. We will always fight for Dierra when she is threatened, but there is no threat here. We won't fight like this anymore, and we don't want you here. Take your cattle, possessions, and what is left of your family, along with any others willing to go with you, and leave this place."

Gassire gathered up his wives and remaining son, along with his cattle and possessions, and left the city. Many of the warriors of Dierra rode along with him, but some only rode a little way in honor of their hero. Others had decided to join Gassire and brought their wives, children, and belongings and continued on the journey. They traveled a long way through the Sahel, and it was a hard journey.

One night, when they had made camp, Gassire sat next to the fire while all the others slept, thinking of all that had happened and wondering what the future held. Finally, Gassire slept; however, he was awakened by a voice singing. It sounded like his own voice, and it was singing the Dausi, the song of his own deeds and the deeds of Dierra. Trembling, Gassire reached for his lute. It was the lute that was singing the Dausi.

It was then that King Nganamba died, at the moment that Gassire's lute began to sing, and it was then that Wagadu fell for the first time. All the anger flooded out of Gassire, and he wept.

Finally, Gassire was at peace.

Part II: Queens and Heroines

Queen Moremi Saves Her People
(Yoruba, Nigeria)

Like Oranyan, Moremi was a historical personage, and the tale retold below has its basis in a historical conflict between the Yoruba and a neighboring tribe. The Edi Festival in Nigeria is celebrated in honor of Moremi's sacrifice every year, and in 2017, a statue of her was erected in the royal palace of Oba Ogunwusi, the Ooni, or traditional ruler, of the Yoruba people. Queen Moremi's life and deeds have also been commemorated in the naming of buildings and in a 2019 musical.

In the days when Oranyan was king over all Ilé-Ifè, there was a woman named Moremi. Moremi was very beautiful and clever, so Oranyan took her as his wife. They lived together in peace for many years, but suddenly, the city of Ilé-Ifè was assailed by swarms of what seemed to be forest spirits. These spirits invaded the farms and the pastures, stealing crops and cattle. They invaded the houses of the town, stealing jewelry and precious carvings. And no one would stand against them because everyone was afraid of them.

"Who can stand against spirits?" the people asked. "We must resign ourselves to our fate. We must run away into the bush and wait until the spirits have passed."

Now, this invasion of spirits did not happen once. It did not happen twice. It happened many, many times, and soon the people of Ilé-Ifè had become poor and hungry, where once they had been wealthy and well-fed. No matter how many prayers the people said or sacrifices they made, the invasion of spirits continued.

Everyone remained afraid of the spirits, everyone, that is, except for Queen Moremi.

She went to her husband and said, "Why don't you take your warriors and fight these spirits? You are Oranyan. We are Ilé-Ifè. We could have made those spirits leave long ago."

"My wife," Oranyan replied. "All of my warriors flee into the bush when the spirits come, and even I can't fight an entire army of spirits all by myself. We will just have to work harder and produce even more food. Perhaps someday we will find a way to make them stop."

"But are they even really spirits? Where do they come from? Where do they take all that food? Surely spirits don't need all of our crops and cattle and wealth. We must find out more about them, and then maybe we will be able to stop them."

"Yes, maybe we will. But how will we do this?"

"I will do it. The next time the spirits come, I will remain here in Ilé-Ifè. They will take me captive. When I discover their secrets, I will return and tell you everything. Then you will know how to save Ilé-Ifè."

At first, Oranyan refused. "What you propose is too dangerous. What if they kill you?"

"Ilé-Ifè is dying anyway. I may as well die trying to help my country rather than starving in it."

Oranyan brought Moremi's proposal to the elders, and they all agreed that this was the best plan, even though it was both perilous and unlikely to work. Moremi then went to the Esimirin River and spoke to the spirit who lived in the waters.

"O spirit," she said. "I ask your help and protection as I try to save my people. If you help me, I will give you a rich sacrifice."

The river spirit appeared and replied, "I will help you if you give me your first-born son, Elu."

Moremi reluctantly agreed, knowing that she would never change the spirit's mind and unlikely be successful without the spirit's help and protection.

The next time the bad spirits invaded Ilé-Ifè, all the people fled except Moremi. She waited in the marketplace for the spirits to come. When they arrived and found her there alone, they scooped her up and carried her out of the city along with everything else they had looted. The spirits ran with Moremi and their loot to a city called Ilé-Igbo. They gave Moremi to their king to be a slave, but because she was so gracious and beautiful, the king soon made her his wife.

It did not take long before Moremi learned the secret of the so-called spirits. They and their king were none other than ordinary men who put on masks and costumes made of raffia fiber that made them look exactly like Egungúns, the spirits of the dead. Because the costumes were so flammable, the men who wore them were extremely careful to avoid any open flames. Now Moremi knew how the "spirits" could be defeated. The next thing she had to do was escape and make her way back home.

One night, when everyone was asleep, Moremi slipped silently out of Ilé-Igbo and began the long journey to her home. When she arrived back in Ilé-Ifè, the people were overjoyed to see her. They ran to tell Oranyan that his beloved wife had returned.

"I know how Ilé-Ifè might be saved," Moremi said. "The 'spirits' who have been raiding us are not supernatural beings. They are human, just like us, from a city called Ilé-Igbo. The raiders look like spirits because they are wearing costumes, which is their weakness. Next time these 'spirits' come to our city, instead of running away, let us all stay hidden here until the raiders enter the city. Let everyone carry a lit torch. Set the raiders' costumes alight, and thus we will defeat our enemies."

The next time the raiders from Ilé-Igbo came to Ilé-Ifè, the people were ready. They allowed the raiders to enter their farmland and city, but instead of running away, they took their torches and lit the raiders' costumes on fire. Only a few of the raiders escaped to tell their king what had happened, but from that day forward, Ilé-Igbo never attacked Ilé-Ifè ever again.

The people of Ilé-Ifè held a great festival to celebrate their victory, but it was a festival tinged with sorrow, for Moremi had pledged to sacrifice her son to the spirit of the river in thanks for the spirit's protection and help. When the festival was over, Moremi took her son Elu to the banks of the river and sacrificed him there. All of Ilé-Ifè came to the river to witness this, and everyone wept with grief over the boy's death—although none grieved harder than Moremi herself.

The boy's body was left there on the river banks while all the people returned home. However, that night, when no one was left by the riverside, a long, golden chain came snaking down from the heavens. It reached all the way down to the ground next to little Elu's body, and no sooner had it done so than Elu's wounds were healed, and he came back to life. Elu climbed up the golden chain and went to live in the heavens with the gods.

Nana Miriam *(Songhai, Mali and Niger)*

In Songhai myth, Nana Miriam is the daughter and granddaughter of giants. Her grandfather, Owadia, is the mythical ancestor of the Songhai peoples of the Niger River Valley.

This story centers on Nana Miriam's defeat of a monstrous hippopotamus ravaging the land. The hippopotamus of today, while not a magical beast with fire along its back, is an extremely dangerous animal known for attacking and killing watercraft, people, and occasionally livestock.

Once there was a man named Fara Maka. Fara Maka was extraordinarily ugly. He was also extraordinarily tall. Fara Maka knew all kinds of magic and other important things, which he taught to his daughter, Nana Miriam, who was also very tall—and very clever.

Now, there came a time when a monstrous hippopotamus was ravaging the people's rice fields. The hippo would come out of the river at night, eat all the rice plants, and then slide back into the river. If this had been an ordinary hippopotamus, dealing with it would have been an easy matter for a strong hunter, but this was no ordinary hippopotamus. It was a magical hippo. It could change its shape. It could make fires burn on its neck and back without being harmed. No matter what the people tried, they could not kill the hippo.

Fara Maka decided to try his luck at killing the hippo. He hunted the beast down and hurled spear after spear at it, but the spears either burnt up in the fires on the hippo's body or the hippo simply swallowed them whole. In the end, Fara Maka had to run away before the hippo swallowed him, too.

We need to find an even mightier hunter than myself to kill that beast, Fara Maka thought.

And so he went to find Kara-digi-Mao-Fosi-Fasi, the greatest hunter in the world. Kara-digi-Mao-Fosi-Fasi was famous for having a pack of one hundred and twenty hunting dogs. These were special hounds, each as large as a horse and twice as fierce as a lion. Kara-digi-Mao-Fosi-Fasi came with his dogs in answer to Fara Maka's summons.

"I will make a good meal for each of your dogs," Fara Maka said. "I want them to be strong and brave when they go out to hunt that hippopotamus."

Kara-digi-Mao-Fosi-Fasi agreed to this. Fara Maka fed each dog a fine meal and then made sure they had comfortable places to sleep. In the morning, Kara-digi-Mao-Fosi-Fasi took his hunting pack down to the river to hunt the hippopotamus. It was not long before he and his dogs found the monstrous beast. One after the other, the dogs leaped at the hippopotamus, trying to bring it down, and one after the other, the hippopotamus swallowed the dogs whole. When all one hundred and twenty dogs had been eaten, the hippopotamus lumbered over to a neighboring rice field and ate everything there as well.

Fara Maka went home crestfallen. He sat down in the shade of a tree near his house, feeling very sorry for himself indeed. Nana Miriam saw him sitting there and went to sit down beside him.

"Father, what is wrong?" Nana Miriam asked.

"It's that beast of a hippopotamus," Fara Maka replied. "I tried to kill it with my spears, but that was no use. Then Kara-digi-Mao-Fosi-Fasi set his dogs on it, but the hippo just ate them and then ate a whole rice field. If we don't get rid of that monster, we'll have no rice to eat, and we will all surely starve."

"Never fear, father. I will see to the hippo."

Nana Miriam went down to the river, where the monstrous hippopotamus was bathing leisurely in the water.

When the hippo saw Nana Miriam watching it from the riverbank, it walked up to her and said, "Greetings, Nana Miriam. I know why you're here. You think you're going to get rid of me. You won't, you know. I ate all of your father's spears. I ate all of Kara-digi-Mao-Fosi-Fasi's dogs. No one can kill me. You may as well go home."

"No one can kill you, you say," Nana Miriam replied. "Well, we'll just have to see about that. Prepare yourself for battle."

In answer, the hippopotamus caused a great ring of fire to leap up around it. Nana Miriam jumped back to avoid the flames, but she was unhurt. Nana Miriam reached into her bag and brought out some magical powder. She said a magic spell and tossed the powder onto the fire, which immediately turned into a puddle of water.

"Not bad, little girl," the hippo said. "But let's see what you can do with iron."

Before Nana Miriam could answer, a great iron wall sprang up, surrounding the hippo. Nana Miriam turned herself into a blacksmith, and using her anvil and other tools, she soon smashed down the iron wall. At this, the hippopotamus became frightened. It tried to run away by turning itself into a creek that would flow into a nearby stream, for it could not run very fast in hippo form. However, no sooner had the hippo-creek flowed into the stream than Nana Miriam threw another magic powder into the water. The stream dried up, leaving the hippopotamus standing there undefended.

The hippo turned tail and ran as fast as it could toward the Niger River, but before the animal could plunge into the water and escape, Nana Miriam made a great wall rise up between the hippo and the river. The hippo turned to run along the wall toward Fara Maka's house. Nana Miriam saw that her father was standing there, waiting to capture the beast; however, before he could grab hold of it, Nana Miriam seized it by one of its back feet, swung it over her head three times, and hurled it as far away as she could. The hippopotamus flew so far that if you wanted to go to where it landed, you would have to travel for ten years.

When Fara Maka saw what Nana Miriam had done, he said, "Well done, my daughter! Well done, indeed! The bards will sing of this deed for years to come!"

Fara Maka made good on his word. He told the bards the story of Nana Miriam's battle with the hippopotamus, and they made a fine song of it. Soon, everyone throughout the land was singing the song of Nana Miriam and the hippopotamus.

However, Nana Miriam herself thought her task was incomplete. The river was still full of hippos, and who knew which of them might become a danger next? Also, the rice harvest had been severely depleted by the monstrous hippo, so the people needed a lot of food—and quickly. Nana Miriam, therefore, sent word throughout the land that meat would be supplied in great plenty soon, that the hunters could leave their bows and spears at home, and that all people would need to do was to come to the river on a certain day, ready to carry the meat away to be prepared.

On the day she had set, Nana Miriam went to Fara Maka and said, "Father, I need an egg."

Fara Maka gave Nana Miriam the egg. Nana Miriam went to the banks of the river, where she cracked the egg, spoke a magic spell into it, and threw it into the water. The water began to fume and roil, and soon dead hippopotami were washing up on the shores of the river. This happened along a great stretch of the river, all the way between Gao and Sansanding. There were so many dead hippos that the people were hard put to collect all the meat.

Now, one of the hippos who lived in the Niger River had been away and not in the water when Nana Miriam threw in the egg, so this hippo was still alive. Moreover, she was heavy with young and about to give birth. Nana Miriam heard that this one hippo was still alive, so she went to her father and asked for another egg.

"Why do you want another egg?" Fara Maka asked.

"There is one hippo left to kill," Nana Miriam replied.

"If you kill that one, then we'll never have any more hippo meat to eat in the future. Let it be."

"Very well."

Word came to the hippo that Nana Miriam had spared its life, so it walked all the way to Fara Maka's house and asked to speak to Nana Miriam.

"I heard you wanted to kill me but that you have spared my life," the hippo said. "Will you let me continue to live?"

"I will," Nana Miriam replied. "You can go where you need to go and live your life."

And so the hippopotamus went down into the river, and she is the ancestor of all the hippos that live today. Also, when hunters go out to catch hippos to eat, they say a charm to bring them a good hunt, and the charm always includes the name of Nana Miriam.

The Maiden and the Fish (*Hausa, Nigeria*)

In this Hausa version of the Cinderella tale, it is a fish that acts as the protagonist's fairy godmother, helping her to marry the king and gain great wealth. Although the protagonist's stepmother is the usual wicked sort found in fairytales the world over, the stepsister here is an honest girl who does not try to take honors she knows do not belong to her, despite her mother's prompting to do so. However, leaving her stepmother's household does not entirely end the young woman's woes, at least not at first; she has to deal with bullying and torture from her co-wives, problems that can only be solved by her magical fish friend.

Once there was a man who had one wife and two daughters. The wife was the mother of one of the daughters and the stepmother of the other, whose own mother had died some time ago. One day, the man went down to the river to fish. He caught a fine, fat fish and brought it home for his wife to cook.

The wife took the fish, handed it to her stepdaughter, and said, "Take this fish down to the river and wash it well. Mind you, don't let it go! That's our dinner, and if you come back empty-handed, I will beat you!"

The stepdaughter took the fish down to the river. She set it in the water and began washing it when suddenly the fish spoke.

The fish said, "Oh, please, please, don't eat me! Please let me go! I have children to feed!"

The young woman took pity on the fish and its hungry children, so she let the fish go. The fish swam away, but the young woman stayed on the banks of the river, waiting. A little while later, the fish came swimming back.

It poked its head above the water and said, "I'm done feeding my children. You can take me home and eat me now."

The young woman was astonished to see the fish had returned. "No, I won't take you. You can go free. Go back to your children."

The fish replied, "Thank you. I will go home now, but you should come back to this spot tomorrow."

Then the fish went back under the water and swam away.

The young woman went home, and when her stepmother saw that she had let the fish go, she beat the girl severely, not stopping until the girl's father said, "Leave her be. We can always get more fish tomorrow."

The next day, the young woman went to the river bank where she had let the fish go. She waited, wondering why the fish had asked her to come back. After a few moments, she saw a whole school of fish swimming toward her, led by the fish she had let go yesterday.

The fish turned to address the others in the school, saying, "See that young woman standing on the riverbank? She's the one who saved my life. She let me go instead of taking me home to eat me. I brought you all here so that you could thank her." Then the fish turned to the young woman and said, "Go home now, but come back on the first night of the festival that follows Ramadan."

On the night of the festival, the stepmother gave her own daughter new clothes and other finery to wear, but to her stepdaughter, she gave only old, ragged clothes. Everyone went to the festival to dance and celebrate, except the young woman, who was ashamed of her ragged clothes. Remembering the fish's request, the young woman went down to the riverbank and waited.

"You seem sad, friend," the fish said to the maiden.

"Everyone has gone to the festival wearing their finest clothes," the young woman replied. "But my stepmother only gave me these old rags. I'm ashamed to be seen."

"Wait here," the fish said.

The fish dove beneath the water and swam away. When the fish returned, it had fine, new clothes for the young woman to wear and a heap of shining jewelry. The young woman put on the finery, thanked the fish, and ran off to join the festival with the others.

Now, the young woman was very beautiful in her own right, but wearing the finery the fish had given her, she looked especially lovely as she danced and laughed at the festival. So beautiful was she that she caught the king's eye.

"I want to marry her," the king said, so he sent a messenger to give the young woman his proposal.

When the messenger had told the girl that the king wished to marry her, she replied, "Very well, but I'm a good girl, and I was raised properly. If his majesty wants to marry me, he must send his messengers to my father's house to speak with him."

The next day, the king's messengers went to the father's house. "We are here because the king wants to marry your daughter."

The father was puzzled by this. "I don't understand. My daughters aren't that special. Why would the king want to marry one of them?"

The stepmother overheard this conversation and said to her own daughter, "The king wants to marry you!"

The daughter replied, "No, he doesn't want to marry me. I saw his messengers talking to another girl. I think it's her that he wants to marry, but I don't know who she is."

She said this because when her stepsister was dressed in the fish's finery, she was so lovely that even her family did not recognize her.

Meanwhile, the father went out and found the daughter who had befriended the fish. When he learned that the messengers had already made the proposal at the festival, he was surprised, but he gave his consent for her to go and be married to the king.

On the night of the wedding, the young woman slipped away from her husband and went to the riverbank.

"Fish! Fish!" she called, and the fish came to the water's edge.

"What is it, friend?" the fish asked.

"I have been married to the king!"

"Allah be praised! Go back to the king's house now, but come back tomorrow." The young woman returned home, but the fish went to all its relatives and said, "My friend has been married to the king! We need to give her gifts to celebrate her wedding."

And so all the fish collected up a great heap of grain and many bolts of fine cloth, and when the young woman came to the riverbank as the fish had asked her to, they gave her all these things.

Now, the young woman was not the king's first wife. He had several other wives, and they were jealous of the young woman's beauty. When the young woman came home with the cloth and the grain the fish had given her, they became even more jealous, so they took her outside and cut off her hands. They laughed at her because now she was mutilated, and they went about the town spreading rumors that the king's new bride was useless because she had no hands.

That night, the young woman told her servant to go to the river and inform the fish what had happened.

The fish said, "My friend saved my life. I will save her hands."

So the fish called together all its relatives, and together, they went to the king's house in secret and gave the young woman her hands back.

In the morning, the king's wives went out to pound sorghum.

"Let's call the king's new bride to come and help us," they said, thinking of humiliating her for not being able to work anymore.

But when the young woman came out of the house and took her turn at the pestle, everyone saw that she had both of her hands.

The townspeople began to laugh at the king's jealous wives, saying, "That's some story you told us about her not having hands! Seems like she has both her hands right where they ought to be!"

From then on, the king's jealous wives did not dare harass the young woman again, and she paid them no mind whatever. The young woman lived a long and happy life with her husband and children, and she never forgot the kindness of her friend, the fish.

The Man-Eating Drum
(*Ikom region, Nigeria*)

The story retold below was originally collected from a woman named Ewonkom in the early twentieth century by Elphinstone Dayrell, who was a British colonial district commissioner in Southern Nigeria. The story comes from Ikom, a town along the Cross River in Southeastern Nigeria.

The drums in the story fit the description of slit drums, which are made by hollowing out a tree trunk and carving a slit in the top so that the hollowed-out trunk can resonate when struck with a stick or a mallet. Such drums are used by the Igbo people of Southeastern Nigeria. Small slit drums are called ekwe and may be small enough to be carried in the hands. Larger drums, called ikoro, can be large enough to hold several fully-grown men inside and may require the player to climb a ladder to play it. Ikoro drums are used primarily for sending messages since they make a loud sound that can carry a great distance.

Ikoro drums are often decorated with bas-relief human figures. There are several legends involving humans being sacrificed to the deity who is thought to live inside the drum. In the story retold below, the drum tries to eat its fill of humans but is foiled by a brave and loving mother who insists on rescuing her daughter.

Long ago, there was a time when the people of Ikom did not know about making drums out of a hollowed-out tree trunk with a slit in it. They did not know that such drums could be used to carry messages a long distance away. They did not know that such drums could make music for dancing, signal to workers that it was time to come home, and sound the alarm if enemies were coming.

Nevertheless, such drums existed, and one of them was named Ndofu. Ndofu was a particularly large drum that lived not far from Ikom and had an evil heart. He liked nothing better than to swallow people and animals whole and hold them hostage in his belly. At first, the people of Ikom did not understand why some of their friends and family did not come home from the bush; however, eventually, they learned that it was because Ndofu had eaten them. From then on, the people of Ikom did not let their children go out alone to help with the farms because it was likely that Ndofu would swallow them, and they would never be heard from again.

At this time, a man named Okongo Osim was living in Ikom. He lived with his wife, Inkang Ezen, and their daughter, Ibanang Okpong.

"You must never go into the bush or go to the farms by yourself, Ibanang," the girl's parents said. "There is an evil being who lives there, and he will eat you right up! No, you must stay here at home where you are safe."

Now, Ibanang thought her parents were being overly cautious, and she chafed at never being allowed to leave her house. Her parents always arranged that one of them would stay home with Ibanang while the other went to the farms, so Ibanang had little chance to slip away.

Ibanang pestered her parents about the farms, saying, "Why can't I go with you? I want to see the farms! It's so boring here!"

But no matter how Ibanang begged, her parents would not let her go to the farms, and so Ibanang became increasingly bored and frustrated by the day.

Now, Ibanang had chores to do around the house, and one of those chores was going to the river to fetch water. One day, it was Okongo's turn to stay home with Ibanang while his wife went to the farms.

Ibanang said to her father, "I'm going to the river to fetch water."

And her father gave her permission to go.

Ibanang picked up her water jar and headed out the door; however, instead of going to the river, she put down her pot and ran down the path she had seen her parents taking to get to the farms.

"I don't care what my parents say," Ibanang said. "I'm a big girl, and I can take care of myself. I'm going to go and help on the farm today, and my parents will see that they are just being silly."

It did not take long before Ibanang came to a fork in the path, but because she had never been to the farms with her parents, she didn't know which one to take.

Maybe I should take the right fork, she thought, and off she went down the right fork of the path.

She ran down the path, and soon she came across a man who was lame sitting under a tree.

"Greetings," the man said. "Can I offer you a kola nut?"

"No, thank you," Ibanang replied, running past the man without stopping. "I'm on the way to the farms to help my mother."

"That's not the way to the farms!" the lame man called, but Ibanang had already run far enough down the path that she didn't hear him.

Ibanang ran on and on, wondering when she would get to the farms. Finally, she found herself out of breath, so she stopped to rest. While she was resting, a small wooden drum came up to her.

"Would you like a kola nut?" the drum asked.

"No, thank you," Ibanang replied. "I'm on the way to the farms to help my mother."

"You're going the wrong way. You need to go back the way you came."

"I think I know where my family's farm is, thank you. Now, if you'll excuse me, I need to go. My mother is waiting for me."

Ibanang continued her journey down the path. Every once in a while, she would come across a drum, each bigger than the last. The drums offered her a kola nut and told her she was going the wrong way, but Ibanang stubbornly refused to listen. Ibanang ran on and on until she came to a clearing in the forest. There, in the middle of the clearing, stood an enormous drum that was held off the ground by a wooden frame. Ibanang stopped in her tracks. She had never seen such a large drum.

"Who are you, and what are you doing here?" the drum asked. "Don't you know that whoever comes here is never allowed to go back?"

Ibanang was frightened. She turned to run away; however, the path was gone. The trees and brush had all moved behind her without her knowing, and there were no other paths she could see in any direction. As Ibanang stood there trying to figure out how to escape, she realized she could hear singing and dancing. She looked around the clearing and as far into the trees as she could see, but no one was there. Soon she realized that the sound was coming from inside the drum. When she moved closer to investigate, the drum opened its giant mouth and swallowed her whole! The girl slid down the inside of the drum and landed in the middle of a big compound full of other people singing and dancing.

Ibanang walked up to one of the dancers and asked, "Where are we? Who are all these people?"

"We are inside the drum," the dancer replied. "We are all the people the drum has been swallowing all these years."

"Why do you stay here? Why don't you just leave?"

"The drum won't let us out. We can only escape if we cut out the drum's heart and liver, but down here, we don't have any knives or machetes to do that with."

When Ibanang realized she was stuck inside the drum for good, she decided to dance and sing with the others, even though she missed her parents and wanted very much to go home.

Later that day, Ibanang's mother returned to the house to find only her husband.

"Where is Ibanang?" she asked.

"She went to the river to draw water," Okongo replied. "But when I went to check on her later, I found the water pot by the path that leads to the farms. I thought she must have gone to the farms to find you. Isn't she with you?"

"No. She must have lost her way. I fear she went to the place where the evil drum lives and has been devoured. How could you let her out of your sight?"

Inkang spent the rest of the night crying.

In the morning, she went to her husband and said, "In three days, I am going to go look for our daughter. If I don't find her, I'm never coming back."

Then Inkang went to her neighbors and borrowed knives and razors from them. She took the knives and razors to the blacksmith and asked him to make them as sharp as possible.

Then she wrapped the knives and razors in a cloth and searched for Ibanang.

Inkang Ezen walked down the path until she came to the place where the lame man sat.

"Can I offer you a kola nut?" the man asked.

"No, thank you," Inkang replied. "I am looking for my daughter. Maybe you saw her pass this way?"

"Yes, a young woman passed by here a few days ago. She said she was going to the farms, but then she took the wrong path, the one that goes to the town of the man-eating drum. She didn't listen when I told her she was going the wrong way."

Inkang thanked the man for his information and went down the path Ibanang had taken. It didn't take long before Inkang came across a small drum.

"Can I offer you a kola nut?" the drum asked.

"No, thank you," Inkang replied. "I am looking for my daughter. Maybe you saw her pass this way?"

"Yes, a young woman went this way a few days ago. I told her she was going the wrong way, but she didn't listen. You should turn back, too. There's an evil man-eating drum at the end of this path."

Inkang thanked the drum for the information but refused to turn back. She continued down the path, meeting drum after drum, who all said that they had seen Ibanang going that way and told Inkang to turn back.

Finally, she arrived at the clearing where the big drum stood.

"Who are you, and why are you here?" the drum asked.

"I am looking for my daughter. Have you seen her?" Inkang replied, trying to sound brave even though she was very frightened.

"I swallowed a young woman a few days ago, so maybe that was her."

"I want to be with my daughter. Please send me wherever you sent her."

"Very well." The drum opened its mouth and swallowed Inkang whole.

Inkang slid down the drum's gullet and landed in the compound where the people were singing and dancing, just as Ibanang had done. Inkang wandered anxiously through the crowd looking for her daughter. It didn't take long before mother and daughter spotted one another. They ran to each other and held one another in a long embrace. The other people noticed the two women embracing and came up to them to see what was going on.

"This is my daughter," Inkang said. "I came to rescue her from the drum. If we work together, we can all escape." Inkang opened the cloth she was carrying and showed the others all the sharp knives and razors. "Take these and cut out the drum's heart and liver. Then we will be able to escape."

The men took the knives and razors and climbed up the drum's insides until they reached where the heart and liver were and started cutting away.

While the men were cutting, the drum shouted, "Oh! Oh! I have such a pain in my inside!"

The drum shouted so loudly that the lame man and all the smaller drums on the path came to see what was wrong.

"What is going on?" the lame man asked. "Why are you crying?"

"I think all the people I swallowed got a knife somehow, and they are trying to cut out my heart and liver so they can escape," the big drum replied. "It hurts so very badly! Please help me!"

But the lame man and the smaller drums said, "We are sorry. We cannot help you."

Finally, the people inside the drum had cut away the drum's heart and liver. The drum fell over, dead. The people then went about cutting a hole in the drum's lips, making a space wide enough for a person to crawl out of. When the hole was made, one man went first to see what things were like outside.

"It's daytime!" he said. "Come out and see the sun!"

The people then climbed out of the drum, taking with them all the animals that the drum had also swallowed.

The people gathered around Inkang Ezen and said, "Thank you for saving us! We can go home to our families now because of you. Please, show us where your house is so that we can visit you from time to time."

Inkang Ezen then took the people to her house and introduced them to her husband. She told him and all the other people in the village that the big man-eating drum was now dead. The chief of the village then sent a group of men with big machetes to hack the drum into pieces and bring it back to the village. The people cooked and ate the flesh of the drum. Then they took the long bones and took out the marrow, and each person took some of the bones home with them, where they made large drums like the one that had eaten them, and they used the bones to beat the drum.

Kumba and Kambili (*Mandinka, Mali*)

Like many legends and folk tales, the story of Kumba and Kambili is a work of fiction whose setting is linked with a historical personage. Imam Samory Touré (c. 1828–1900), who plays the role of the ruler in the story retold below, was a Muslim cleric and leader of the Wassoulou Empire in Mali in the late nineteenth century. The tale of Kumba and Kambili has no historical authenticity; Samory Touré is merely used as a device to anchor the story in time and place.

The story presented below is based on a version of the legend told to linguist Charles S. Bird in 1968 by the Mandinka jeli Seydou Camara. A jeli, or griot, holds an important place in Malian society. Jelis act as repositories of their people's history and stories and have an important function in singing the praises of heroes, warriors, leaders, and other important people. They may also be called upon to advise rulers and other leaders. A jeli plays a role at the end of this tale as well by being tasked with creating a praise song for Kumba in celebration of her bravery and cunning in helping bring down the evil sorcerer who is the villain of the piece.

The great Imam Samory Touré had a general named Kanji. Kanji was a brave warrior; however, he was sad that he had no children, for none of his nine wives had ever been able to conceive.

Kanji went to Samory Touré and said, "Imam, can you or your holy men tell me whether I will ever have a son? None of my wives have yet borne children, and I fear I will go to my grave without children."

Samory Touré gathered all the holy men and asked them to divine whether Kanji would ever have a son. The holy men performed their divinations, and one by one, they saw that Kanji would have a great son, but none of them could say which wife would be the mother.

Finally, there was only one holy man left to cast his divination.

This one looked at Kanji and said, "You will have a son. He will be very brave and a fine hunter. He will be born of your wife named Dugo."

"But Dugo is despised by my chief wife," Kanji replied. "If my chief wife finds out about this, she will kill Dugo, and my other wives will help her do it because they also hate Dugo."

"Bring your wives to me," the holy man said. "I will help you with this."

Kanji summoned his wives and brought them before the holy man.

"I understand that none of you have yet borne a child. If you are to become mothers, you must not have relations with your husband for a full month," the holy man said.

That night, the holy man crept into the hut in the goat pen, to which Dugo had been banished by Kanji's chief wife.

"Come with me," the holy man said.

Dugo followed him to Kanji's house, where the holy man told her to have relations with her husband. Every night for a month, the holy man came to Dugo's house and stealthily brought her to her husband, bringing her back each morning before daybreak.

It was not long before Dugo found herself with child. The other wives were incredulous, and the chief wife was especially envious.

"How is it that you got yourself with child? Have you been having relations with a goat? Or have you been sneaking into our husband's house at night?" the chief wife asked.

However, Dugo gave her no answer.

Furious, the chief wife went to see Samory Touré. "O Imam, how is it that Dugo is pregnant when the holy man told us that we were to stay out of our husband's bed for a whole month? Dugo must be having relations with the goats, and she must be punished."

Samory Touré replied, "That is a serious accusation to make, but I won't pass judgment until the child is born. What should your punishment be if it turns out you have been telling bad stories about Dugo and that the father of her child is a man and not a goat?"

"I will sweep your compound with my buttocks," the chief wife replied.

Now, Dugo's pregnancy was not an easy one. Her co-wives shunned her even more than they had before because they were all jealous that she was to be the bearer of the first child. All the dirtiest tasks were given to Dugo. But more than that, her baby kept trying to leave her womb before it was time. Even so, somehow, Dugo managed to keep her baby inside until her nine months had passed, and she finally delivered a beautiful baby boy. When Kanji, the Imam, and the co-wives came to see Dugo and her baby named Kambili, they all agreed that he looked like a small version of Kanji. And so it was that the chief wife had to go and sweep the Imam's courtyard with her buttocks as punishment for telling bad stories about Dugo.

Kambili grew quickly, for his mother cared for him well. Dugo had been brought back to Kanji's compound and given a proper house in which to raise the child. All of the co-wives were still envious; however, none more than the chief wife, who not only had the shame of not being the first to bear a child but had also endured the humiliation of her punishment for telling tales about Dugo. One night, the chief wife decided she would get her revenge by killing the child. She took a knife and crept into Dugo's house in the night, thinking to cut the child's throat while he and Dugo slept. Yet, unbeknownst to the chief wife, Kanji happened to be there visiting Dugo and the baby, and before the chief wife could do any harm, Kanji killed her. From that night forward, Dugo became Kanji's favored wife.

Kambili grew into a strong lad who was swift of foot. He became an expert hunter, wielding spear, bow, and rifle with equal skill. No animal was safe from Kambili when he was on a hunt. He always came back laden with meat for his family to eat and share with others who had need.

A young woman named Kumba also lived in Kambili's village. Kumba and Kambili had been friends since they were children, and when they came of age to marry, Kambili decided to ask Kumba to be his wife.

"Oh, Kambili," Kumba replied when Kambili had asked her. "I do want to be your wife, but I am promised to Cekura. Cekura is a powerful sorcerer. If I do not marry him, he will be very angry and take his revenge not only on us but on our whole village."

"If he hurts anyone, we will kill him," Kambili said. "The two of us are more than a match for him."

And so it was that Kumba and Kambili were married in a joyful ceremony with much singing and dancing. As Kumba had foretold, Cekura was furious that Kumba had married another and decided to take his revenge starting the next day. Cekura transformed into a lion and went into the village, where he pounced on a man and dragged him away into the bush. The next day, he did the same, taking a woman this time. Soon, all the village people were afraid to leave their homes. Samory Touré was angry that this lion had been terrorizing his people. He called all the hunters and demanded they find this man-eating lion and kill it.

Kambili went home and told Kumba about Samory's command that the lion be killed.

"Samory is right," Kumba said. "That lion should be killed. But it's no ordinary lion. That is Cekura in disguise. Cekura knows how to transform himself into different animals and has magical protection. We will need magic if we are to defeat him."

Kambili agreed with Kumba, so they went to visit a holy man to ask him to divine what they needed to kill Cekura.

When the holy man had performed his divination, he said, "You need to get some hair from him, some from his head, arm, and private place. Bring me also one of his sandals and an old pair of his trousers."

Kumba said to Kambili, "I need to be the one to do this. Cekura will never let you near him, but I can pretend that I would have preferred to marry him and fool him long enough to get the hair and the other things." Kambili was afraid that Cekura would harm Kumba, but she added, "Never fear, husband. I will return home safely. Trust me, trust my courage."

And so Kumba took some kola nuts and other appropriate gifts and put them into calabashes to take to Cekura as part of her plan to convince him that she wanted to be with him. She went to Cekura's home and found him sitting outside under a tree.

"Well, well, well, if it isn't Kumba, the hunter's wife!" Cekura said. "Whatever are you doing here? Shouldn't you be with your famous husband?"

"I have decided that being a hunter's wife isn't for me," Kumba replied. "It was a mistake to have married him. I should have stayed with you. Maybe we can get rid of Kambili and then be together at last."

Cekura invited Kumba into the house, where his mother prepared a meal for her. That night, Kumba got into bed with Cekura. When Cekura tried to make love to her, she pushed him away.

"Why are you refusing me?" he asked. "I thought you said you wanted to be with me."

"Oh, I do," Kumba replied. "But first, we need to kill Kambili. He's very strong, you know, and has strong magic, so we'll need to use magic of our own to do the deed."

"Tell me what you need for the spell, and it is yours."

"I need hairs from your head, arm, and private place. I also need one of your sandals and an old pair of your trousers. Then I can make the magic that will kill Kambili."

Cekura gave Kumba everything she needed. She put all the items into a calabash and then made ready to leave.

"I can't wait to see you again, Cekura," she said.

"I can't wait to have you back," Cekura replied. "Now, mind you, don't betray me!"

"I would never do that!"

Kumba left and walked back to her home. When she returned to her village, she went to the diviner and gave him the calabash. The diviner took the calabash and used it to make the magic that would be Cekura's downfall. Then he buried it at the foot of a tree in the village marketplace.

Meanwhile, Kambili went out into the bush and did some hunter's divination of his own. He summoned a spirit that told him to make his blind in the tree that stood in the marketplace.

However, before setting up his blind, Kambili went to Samory Touré and said, "I am setting up a blind in the tree in the marketplace so that I can kill the man-eating lion. But I'll need bait for the trap. I need a young boy to be tied to the base of the tree to lure the lion to me."

Samory Touré agreed that this was a good plan and arranged for a young boy to go with Kambili.

As the boy was being tied to the tree, Kumba gave him an amulet.

"Wear this around your neck, and nothing will harm you," Kumba said. Then Kumba said to Kambili, "Climb into your blind. I will go and get Cekura. He thinks that we are going to kill you, but I know you will kill him first."

Cekura took the form of a lion and went to the village with Kumba. There he saw the lad tied to the tree. Kambili, lying in his hunter's blind, saw Cekura approaching.

Pretending to be the young boy, Kambili said, "I'm not afraid of you, lion, even though I'm tied up here!"

Cekura hesitated. He had not seen the boy's mouth move when he heard the voice.

"What's the matter? Afraid to eat me?" the voice said again, and then Cekura was sure that someone else was pretending to be the boy.

Cekura circled around the tree, looking and looking until he saw Kambili's blind. Cekura then cast a sleeping spell on Kambili, and powerful as Kambili's magic was, he could not resist Cekura's magic and fell asleep.

When the boy at the foot of the tree realized that Kambili was under a spell, he began to sing.

"Hunter, the prey has arrived!

Hunter, why do you sleep?

Hunter, the prey has arrived!

Hunter, you must awake!"

So powerful was the boy's song that Kambili woke up and saw Cekura standing there in lion form. Kambili raised his rifle, aimed, and took his shot, which hit Cekura square between the eyes, killing him instantly.

When the village people heard the shot, they came to see what had happened. There they found Kumba, Kambili, and the young boy standing over the body of the lion. As they watched, the lion transformed into the body of Cekura, who lay in the dust, dead.

Samory Touré came forward and said, "Is it done? Is the lion truly dead?"

"Truly, he is dead," Kambili replied. "And it is all because of the courage of my wife, Kumba. She made it possible for me to shoot Cekura. And it is because of the courage of the boy, here, who sang me awake when Cekura cast a spell to make me sleep."

"Well done, all of you. I will tell my jeli to make a song of this, the song of Kumba, to be her reward for her bravery. What shall be your reward, Kambili, and what of the boy?"

"Give me the boy to be my apprentice," Kambili said. "He stood before the lion and did not flinch. He has the courage of a true hunter."

Hence, Samory Touré had his jeli make a song for Kumba, made the boy Kambili's apprentice, and gave Kumba and Kambili many other gifts.

That night, the village held a great feast, and the jeli sang Kumba's song so everyone would remember what she had done for her people.

Part III: Spirits and Monsters

Kigbo Learns a Lesson (*Yoruba, Nigeria*)

All cultures have fables extolling the virtues of hard work and the vices of laziness and greed, and the Yoruba of Nigeria are no different. In this tale, a man named Kigbo learns that lesson the hard way. He also learns the value of staying away from supernatural beings whose actions he can neither truly predict nor control.

Once there was a young man named Kigbo. He had a lovely wife named Delapo, and they had just welcomed their first child, Ojo. Now, this Kigbo was a very stubborn lad. Once he got an idea into his head, there was no getting it out. No matter how good the advice was, Kigbo would ignore it and do whatever he wanted.

One day, Kigbo's father came to visit Kigbo and Delapo and the baby.

"Kigbo," the father said. "You are a married man now. You have a child. It is time that you started a farm of your own. Tomorrow, let us go to the edge of the village to see whether we can find you a nice plot of land so that you can feed your family yourself."

"Yes, it is time for me to start a farm," Kigbo replied. "But I have a different place in mind."

"Oh? Where would that be?"

"I think I'd like to clear some land in the bush. Most of the land near the village has already been claimed. I want to have a nice big farm, but I won't be able to do that if I farm near the village."

"But you don't need a big farm. You only need something big enough to feed yourself and your family, and the bush is crawling with spirits."

"Yes, I do, and yes, it is. I don't care about spirits. I mean to have my farm out in the bush, and the spirits can help me, or they can get out of my way."

Kigbo's father sighed. He knew that it wasn't worth arguing further. But he was worried about his son. "Kigbo, I know you will do what you want no matter what I or anyone else says. But think carefully about whether it is wise to farm in the bush. The spirits may not be as friendly as you seem to think they will be."

The next day, Kigbo took his tools and went out into the bush. When he found a bit of land that he thought was suitable, he started to clear away the trees and brush. No sooner had he begun his work than a group of spirits appeared.

"This is our land," the spirits said. "What are you doing here with all those tools?"

"I am clearing land for a farm," Kigbo replied.

"You are clearing land where we live. We will do as you do."

And so Kigbo returned to his work, and the spirits helped him. In no time at all, a great patch of land had been cleared. When Kigbo stopped his work, the spirits stopped also, and they disappeared back into the bush.

Well, those spirits certainly were helpful, whatever my father might say, Kigbo thought as he walked back home. *I was right to start my farm here. I'll have no trouble from spirits.*

The next day, Kigbo returned to the land he had cleared to burn the brush that had been cut. As Kigbo was piling the brush up to be burnt, the spirits reappeared.

"This is our land," the spirits said. "Why are you piling up all that brush?"

"I need to burn it so I can farm here," Kigbo replied.

"You are piling and burning brush where we live. We will do as you do."

And so the spirits helped Kigbo pile up all the brush and set it alight. Kigbo and the spirits waited near the great blaze until it was ash, and when the fire was only a heap of glowing coals, the spirits vanished back into the bush, and Kigbo went home.

Kigbo's father saw him returning from the bush, and said, "How are you doing, son? Are you still farming in the bush? Are the spirits giving you any trouble?"

"Quite the contrary," Kigbo replied. "They've been very helpful so far. I shall have the biggest farm of any man for miles around."

Kigbo's father sighed. "The spirits might be helpful now, but that might not always be the case. We are men, and they are spirits, and they live differently from us. They can also hurt you if they choose. I wish you would drop your foolishness and come farm closer to the village."

"Nonsense. I've already done a great deal of work, and I like the place I've cleared. I'm not going to stop now."

In the morning, Kigbo took a bag full of millet seed and set out for his field. When he got to the field, he began sowing the seed. No sooner had he started his work than the spirits appeared once more.

"This is our land," the spirits said. "Why are you sowing that seed?"

"I'm sowing it to grow grain for my family to eat," Kigbo replied.

"You are sowing seed to grow grain where we live. We will do as you do."

And so the spirits helped Kigbo sow his grain, and soon the fields were all planted. When the planting was done, Kigbo decided that he would walk to a neighboring village to visit some friends. He did this without telling anyone else where he was going. At home, his wife Delapo waited for him. At first, she did not worry because Kigbo had gone on journeys before and always came home. However, this time was different. This time, Kigbo was farming in the bush, and there was no telling what the spirits might have done.

Delapo waited for as many days as she could, for as many days as Kigbo had been away before. When he still did not return, she took little Ojo to where Kigbo had planted his crops. There Delapo saw that the millet was growing well; the grain was in the ear, but it was not yet ripe. Delapo looked about, but there was no sign of Kigbo.

Suddenly, Ojo said, "Mama, pick some of that grain for me to eat. I'm hungry."

Delapo picked a stalk of millet and handed it to Ojo.

Just as she did so, the spirits appeared and said, "This is our land. Who are you, and what are you doing?"

"I am Delapo, the wife of Kigbo," Delapo replied. "I am picking a stalk of grain for my little one to eat."

"You are picking a stalk of grain where we live. We will do as you do." Then the spirits set about picking the stalks of millet until not one plant was left standing.

Just then, Kigbo arrived. He saw his wife and all the millet lying on the ground, and he became very angry and frightened.

"What have you done?" he cried. "The millet was not yet ripe! We now have no harvest!"

"The baby said he was hungry, so I picked a stalk of grain for him to eat," Delapo said. "Then a group of spirits came and started picking the grain themselves. I thought you said these bush spirits were helpful!"

"Why did you have to be hungry right now?" Kigbo shouted at his child. "Look what happened!"

The spirits reappeared and said, "You are shouting at your child where we live. We will do as you do," and they began shouting at poor little Ojo until he began to cry.

"Look what happened!" Kigbo said to Delapo. "You picked grain for the child, and then the spirits came and picked all the rest, and now we have no grain to harvest! This is all your fault!"

When the spirits heard Kigbo yelling at his wife, they said, "You are shouting at your wife where we live. We will do as you do," and they began shouting at Delapo, who was very frightened and began crying herself.

"Oh, what have I done?" Kigbo beat his head with his fists. "What have I done? I should have listened to my father!"

Then the spirits said, "You are hitting yourself in the head where we live. We will do as you do," and they started beating Kigbo with their fists. This was too much for Kigbo. He grabbed his wife and child by the hands, and the three of them ran back to the village as fast as they could. Fortunately, the spirits stayed on their land and did not follow Kigbo and his family.

Kigbo's father saw Kigbo, Delapo, and Ojo running toward the village. He saw that Delapo and Ojo were both crying and that Kigbo's face was bruised and bloodied.

"What has happened?" Kigbo's father cried. "What happened to you?"

"It was the bush spirits," Kigbo replied. "You were right. I never should have tried to farm in the bush. I'll never do that again."

"Perhaps tomorrow we can find you a nice plot of land near the village."

"Yes," Kigbo said. "That will do very nicely."

The Tale of Oluronbi

This story involves the spirit of the iroko tree, a hardwood that grows in the forests of West Africa. The tree is both tall and long-lived; some trees are known to have lived for over five hundred years. In the Yoruba culture, this tree is thought to have magical properties and contain a resident spirit that needs to be propitiated, especially if the tree has been cut down for any reason. The wood is versatile and can be used for many building purposes. It is also often used in the making of certain types of drums.

Once there was a village that seemed quite prosperous. All the people lived in nice houses, the farms were fertile, and the herd animals were healthy. However, the village had a sad secret: No children had been born for many years. The men and the women tried and tried to have children, but nothing ever helped. They tried prayers, sacrifices, and medicines, but still, they had no children.

Finally, the women of the village held council together about what they might do to end the apparent curse they were under. They decided they would go to the sacred iroko tree that stood just outside the village and ask the spirit of the tree for help.

The women went up to the tree and said, "O Iroko-man, we plead for your help! No one in our village has had a child for many years, and this makes us all very sorrowful."

The Iroko-man appeared before the women and replied, "If I give you children, what will you give me in return?"

Some women promised yams. Some promised the lambs that would soon be born. Others promised to bring the best calves from their herds. All the women had something precious to give to the Iroko-man, except for a woman named Oluronbi. Oluronbi was the wife of the village woodworker. She and her husband had neither yams nor lambs nor calves to bring; they were very poor.

However, Oluronbi was desperate for a child, so she said, "I will give you my child."

The months passed, and the women all became heavy with child. One by one, they were delivered of fine, healthy children, and each brought the gifts they had promised to the iroko tree. When it came time for Oluronbi to deliver her child, she gave birth to a baby girl. Everyone in the village said that Oluronbi's daughter was the most beautiful baby of all those born in the village that year.

Time passed, and although Oluronbi remembered having made a promise to the Iroko-man, she and her husband loved their daughter so much that they could not bear to part with her. But one day, Oluronbi went into the forest by herself and happened to pass by the iroko tree.

The Iroko-man appeared and said, "All the other women have paid me what they promised. You have not."

And before Oluronbi could reply, the Iroko-man turned her into a small, brown bird.

Now, back in the village, Oluronbi's husband waited for his wife to return. When she did not, he became very worried, so he brought his daughter to his parents' house and set out to find his wife. As the woodworker walked through the forest, he heard the song of a small bird. The bird seemed to be singing words, so he stopped and listened closely. The little bird flew over and alit on a branch just above the woodworker's head and began to sing:

"One promised a lamb,

One promised some yams,

One promised a calf,

But Oluronbi promised her child."

The woodworker listened very closely to the bird's song, and soon he realized that the bird was none other than his beloved Oluronbi. The woodworker sped home as fast as his legs could take him. He took a good log from the pile and began carving it into the likeness of his child. When the statue was done, he put clothing and jewelry on it and took it to the iroko tree. The woodworker laid the doll respectfully at the foot of the tree and went home.

The Iroko-man saw the wooden doll at the foot of his tree and thought, *Aha! Oluronbi has given me her child at last!*

Then the Iroko-man turned Oluronbi back into a woman, snatched up the doll, and disappeared back into his tree.

Bewildered but grateful to be human again, Oluronbi hurried back to her village, where she was joyfully reunited with her husband and child. However, she never went near the sacred iroko tree until the end of her days.

Sasabonsam Meets His Match
(*Sefwi, Ghana*)

The Sefwi are an Akan-speaking people who live in Southwestern Ghana, principally in the Western North Region. The story retold below includes the character of the sasabonsam, a villainous monster who appears in many West African myths and legends. In an article in the online journal Atlas Obscura, *author Nicole Zakheim observes that one important function of the sasabonsam was to enforce rules meant to preserve the environment. In this tale, however, it is unclear whether the hunter is breaking any rules, so the sasabonsam here functions solely as a terrifying monster who must be slain.*

One day a hunter went out with his gun to see whether he might catch anything for himself and his wife to eat. The hunter wandered all day without seeing any game. The sun had begun to set, and the hunter had decided to go home when suddenly he saw a fine antelope. The hunter raised his gun and killed the antelope with one shot. Just as the hunter was trussing the carcass to take home to his wife, he heard a strange voice behind him.

The voice said, "Cut off the legs and give me the rest!"

The hunter turned around and saw something that looked like a man, but it was not a man. It was as tall as a tree, and flames shot out of its eyes. Every one of its teeth was long, pointed, and sharp as the sharpest dagger. The hunter dared not disobey the monster, whose name was Sasabonsam, so he cut off the antelope's legs and tied them together to take home. The monster bent down and took the rest of the antelope, placed it in its mouth, and swallowed it whole. Then it disappeared as though it had never been there at all. When the hunter regained his wits, he went home with the antelope legs and gave them to his wife to prepare.

The next day, the hunter went out to see what he could catch. Again, he shot a fine antelope, and the monster appeared and demanded that the hunter cut off the legs and give him the rest. This repeatedly happened, day after day, until the hunter's wife finally began to wonder what her husband was doing with the rest of the carcasses.

That's fine meat that's going to waste and good hides, horns, and bones, she thought. *I need to find out what my husband is doing in the bush and where the rest is going.*

The wife knew her husband would never let her accompany him on a hunting trip, not least because she was now with child, so she had to find a different way to follow him. Hence that night, when her husband was asleep, she drilled a small hole in the box that held the powder for her husband's rifle, and in the morning, after the husband had left to go hunting, the wife followed the little trail of powder into the bush.

Presently, the hunter caught sight of an antelope and raised his gun to fire. The wife hid behind a tree and watched as the hunter shot the antelope.

The wife heard a voice say, "Cut off the legs and give me the rest!" But when the hunter bent to cut the legs off the antelope, the voice said, "Not that one, this one!"

The hunter turned to see Sasabonsam pointing to the tree where the wife was hiding.

That's odd, the hunter thought, but he dared not disobey the monster, so he went to see what was behind the tree. There the hunter found his wife, who had seen Sasabonsam and had fainted dead away.

"Cut the legs off that one!" Sasabonsam said, pointing to the unconscious woman.

The hunter could not move. He was terrified of what Sasabonsam would do if he did not obey, but he could not harm his wife. Finally, Sasabonsam got tired of waiting. He reached down and picked up the wife, but as he did so, her belly miraculously opened, and a baby jumped out. The baby grew and grew until he was a full-grown man. Then the baby grew some more until it was as tall and broad as Sasabonsam, and like Sasabonsam, the baby now had eyes of flame and dagger-sharp teeth.

The newly born giant roared and rushed at Sasabonsam, who dropped the wife to the ground. The two monsters grunted, snarled, and grappled with one another. They hit each other with their fists. They kicked each other with their feet. They uprooted trees and used them as clubs. The fight continued, with neither giant getting the upper hand, until finally, they both lay on the ground, exhausted.

Sasabonsam was lying there with his eyes closed, but the child-giant was watching his enemy closely. There on Sasabonsam's belt, the child spied a small hammer. The child-giant struck out quick as lightning, grabbing the hammer and hitting Sasabonsam on the head with it three times.

"Nana Nyame Kwame!" Sasabonsam cried. "O great Sky God, come and rescue me! This child-giant is going to kill me!"

However, the Sky God did not listen to Sasabonsam's pleas, and tall as he was, Sasabonsam could not reach the heavens to pull himself up. He fell with a mighty crash, and his body turned into a river, his arms and legs becoming tributary streams flowing into the river. And the child-giant? He shrank down to baby-size and went back into his mother's womb, where he waited to be born. And when he was born, he was given the name Akokoaa Kwasi Gyinamoa.

Zin-Bakaru (*Songhai, Mali and Niger*)

This tale comes from the Songhai people of the Niger River valley. The Songhai live in parts of what are now Mali and Niger and were one of the peoples drawn into the Malian Empire founded by Sunjata. When the Malian empire began to weaken in the fifteenth century, the Songhai established their empire in the Sahel region, which lasted until the end of the sixteenth century.

Although the river spirit in this story is said to play a guitar, it is unlikely that the modern Western instrument is what is meant. It is more likely that this spirit played a traditional West African instrument, such as the kora *or the* n'goni. *The* kora *is a harp with twenty-one strings attached to a long neck set in a large calabash resonator. The* n'goni *is a smaller instrument with four strings that look like a guitar, a narrow, elliptical resonating body and a long, fretless neck.*

Once there was a river spirit who lived in the waters of the Niger River. The spirit's name was Zin-Bakaru. Zin-Bakaru liked nothing better than to play his guitar, for his music gave him power over the fish and animals living there. Not far from where Zin-Bakaru lived, a rice farmer named Faran lived with his elderly mother. Faran was a poor man, made poorer every day because his rice crop kept disappearing before any of it had a chance to be harvested.

Faran did not know what was making his rice crop disappear, so one night, he lay in wait to see who was stealing all his rice. Not long after moonrise, Faran heard the noise of a guitar being played. He looked around and saw the spirit Zin-Bakaru playing the guitar. A rushing sound came from the river, and soon, Faran saw what was making the noise: It was a huge shoal of fish wriggling their way into the rice paddies and making away with the rice. It was in this way that Zin-Bakaru fed himself—by stealing Faran's rice.

Well, if Zin-Bakaru is going to use fish to steal my rice, then I'll go fishing and cut down on the number of thieves, Faran thought.

However, no sooner had Faran taken his canoe out onto the river and cast his nets than Zin-Bakaru played his guitar again, making all the fish swim away. And so Faran and his mother had to go hungry again that night.

"I need to do something about that horrible Zin-Bakaru," Faran told his mother. "In the morning, I'm going to challenge him to a fight."

Faran was as good as his word. He marched down to the river's edge and shouted, "Zin-Bakaru! I know that it's you taking away my rice and scaring away the fish with that guitar of yours. My mother and I are going to starve if you keep that up."

Zin-Bakaru came and stood before Faran and replied, "I don't care if you starve. That's not my problem. And my guitar is mine. Go away."

"I'll fight you for your guitar. If I win, you have to give it to me."

Zin-Bakaru was intrigued. Faran didn't look like much of a fighter, so Zin-Bakaru figured he would win easily.

"All right," Zin-Bakaru said. "But I get your canoe if I win."

"Done."

The man and the spirit went over to a patch of flat, dry ground that lay hard by and began to wrestle. Now, Zin-Bakaru was not wrong that Faran wasn't much of a fighter, but Faran was also desperate and fighting for his life and his mother's. They fought for a long time without either of them gaining the upper hand until suddenly, something shifted, and Zin-Bakaru found he was losing.

I can't possibly lose to a mortal, Zin-Bakaru thought. *I couldn't stand the shame.*

And so Zin-Bakaru decided to cheat by saying a magic word in Faran's ear. No sooner had Zin-Bakaru pronounced the word than Faran went limp, and Zin-Bakaru pronounced himself the victor.

"Thanks for the lovely canoe," Zin-Bakaru said. "Now go back home to your mother, and don't bother me again."

Faran went home, weeping and ashamed. He told his mother what had happened and how Zin-Bakaru had cheated in their fight.

"Use magic on my boy, will he?" Faran's mother said. "Well, we'll see about that. Come here, Faran, and I'll teach you a magic word of your own. Tomorrow, you go back to that scoundrel and challenge him again. If he tries to use magic on you, you just use that word I taught you, and everything will turn out well."

In the morning, Faran borrowed a canoe from his neighbor, promising to bring it back by the end of the day. Now, this canoe was much larger and much finer than Faran's, so Faran hoped that Zin-Bakaru would accept his challenge to win an even better prize than the one he had won yesterday. Faran beached the canoe in the same place he had met Zin-Bakaru and again shouted for the spirit to come out to meet him.

"What, you again?" Zin-Bakaru said. "Didn't you get enough of a drubbing yesterday?"

"I don't care what happened yesterday," Faran replied. "If nobody makes you stop what you're doing, my mother and I will starve. So, I'm here to challenge you to a fight again. If I win, I get my canoe back and your guitar. If you win, you get this canoe here. It's much better than my old canoe, so it will be worth your while to try for it."

Zin-Bakaru, being both greedy and overconfident, said, "Agreed. Shall we fight in the same place we fought yesterday?"

Faran nodded, so the two of them went to the flat, dry place along the riverbank and began their fight. This time, all the other river spirits came out to watch, for Zin-Bakaru had been telling them the story of how he defeated Faran, and the spirits wanted to see him do it again. The man and the spirit fought for a long time. Again, Faran began to get the upper hand, and again Zin-Bakaru spoke his magic word in Faran's ear. However, this time, Faran was prepared: He immediately said his own magic word into Zin-Bakaru's ear, and this time it was the spirit who went limp. Faran had won!

Zin-Bakaru ran to the water and dove in. The other spirits, seeing their leader run away from the fight, also dove into the water, leaving behind all their musical instruments. Faran collected his canoe and all the musical instruments. He went to the place where the spirits kept slaves captive and released them all. Then Faran returned home, returned his neighbor's canoe, and put the water spirits' musical instruments in the home he shared with his mother. Zin-Bakaru, for his part, was so humiliated that he never tried to charm the fish again, so Faran and his mother lived well on the rice from their farm and the fish from the river.

Kwaku Tsin and the Serpent
(*Ashanti, Ghana*)

Tales of the Ashanti spider trickster Kwaku Anansi are well known within West Africa and many other countries. In this tale, however, it is Anansi's son, Kwaku Tsin, who takes center stage as the hero and trickster, showing that this apple does not fall far from the tree.

In Ashanti culture, children are commonly named after the day on which they were born. The forename "Kwaku" means "born on Wednesday." Such names have other associations. For example, the "born on Saturday" names Kofi (masc.) and Efua (fem.) are associated with fertility. In particular, the masculine Kwaku and its feminine counterpart Akua are associated with the spider trickster Anansi.

There came a time when there was a famine in the land, and everyone was very hungry.

One day, Anansi said to his son, Kwaku Tsin, "Let's go hunting. Maybe we can fill our bellies tonight if we can catch something."

And so Anansi and Kwaku Tsin took up their bows and went into the forest to see what game they might find. It was not long before Kwaku Tsin killed a fine deer, and father and son rejoiced that they would eat well that day.

"Wait here while I get a basket to carry the meat home," Anansi said.

"Yes, Father," Kwaku Tsin replied, who stood watchfully over the carcass of the deer.

Minutes passed. And then an hour had gone by.

Our home is not that far away, Kwaku Tsin thought. *What could be keeping my father? Has he gotten lost in the forest?*

Thinking to guide his father to the place where he was waiting, Kwaku Tsin called out, "Father! Father!"

A voice replied, "Yes, Son?"

Thinking this was Anansi, Kwaku Tsin called out again, "I'm over here! Bring the basket!"

However, instead of Anansi, a great serpent slithered out from between the trees. Before the serpent could catch sight of him, Kwaku Tsin ran and hid.

The serpent slithered up to the place where Kwaku Tsin had been standing and said, "Why, it's only a dead deer! I could have sworn there was a man about. Now I shall have no man to eat for my dinner!"

And so the serpent went angrily away.

Not long after the serpent left, Anansi came striding up, carrying a basket.

Kwaku Tsin came out of hiding and said, "Father! It is good to see you are here and well. There was an immense serpent that came when I called out to you, and I'm sure it would have eaten us both on the spot!"

"That was a fine adventure, Son!" Anansi replied. "I wish I had been there to see the beast."

No sooner had Anansi finished speaking than he got his wish: The serpent returned, lured back to the spot by Anansi's scent as Anansi moved through the forest. The serpent pounced on Anansi and his son and took them both to his home, thinking of dining on them later. Anansi and Kwaku Tsin found they were not alone, for the serpent's house was full of many other unfortunate people he was saving to eat later.

Among the creatures was a white rooster, but the rooster was not intended for the serpent's meal. Instead, the rooster was the serpent's jailer and charged with ensuring that none of the captives escaped.

"Here are some more prisoners," the serpent said to the rooster. "Crow loudly if anything unusual happens or the prisoners try to escape."

Then the serpent left to go find more prey to bring home.

Kwaku Tsin gathered together all the captives and said, "Right, how are we getting out of here?"

"Escape is impossible," one of the captives replied. "That rooster crows the minute any of us moves toward the door."

"And even if we did manage to get out, the serpent would smell you or see you and bring you right back, assuming he didn't just eat you on the spot," another said.

"That is bad," Kwaku Tsin said. "But give me some time to think. I'll find a way to get us out."

Kwaku Tsin looked about the serpent's home. He saw some bags of grain and hemp ready to be spun. Out in the cattle pen, he saw some cattle.

He gathered his fellow prisoners and said, "I know what we must do. I'm going to spill that grain on the floor. The rooster won't be able to resist it, and he can't crow while he's eating. While the rooster is eating, some of us must spin that hemp into twine and make a rope ladder of it. We'll toss that up toward the sky, and if we're lucky, the gods will catch it so we can climb up. We also need to kill some cattle and strip them down to the bones. I'll need the bones for my plan."

Kwaku Tsin spilled the grain on the floor, and when the rooster was busy eating, some of the people began to spin the hemp while the others slaughtered some of the cattle and began stripping the flesh off the bones, cooking the meat and giving it to all the prisoners to eat. When the rope ladder and bones were ready, Kwaku Tsin put the bones into a bag and picked up the serpent's fiddle. Then he tossed up the ladder, which miraculously stayed hanging in the air.

"The gods will hold the ladder for you. Climb up as quickly as you can, and do not stop until you reach the heavens," Kwaku Tsin said.

"What will you do?" one of the people asked.

"Don't worry about me. I have to take care of the serpent first. I'll join you when I am able."

Now, the serpent was out hunting, but every once in a while, he would glance back toward his home to see whether everything was in order. This time when he looked, he saw something strange. He saw a long, thin ladder going up to the heavens from outside his house, and his captives were all climbing swiftly upward. The serpent hastened back home just as the last captive began climbing. Kwaku Tsin saw the serpent coming, but before the serpent could catch him, Kwaku Tsin tossed one of the bones from his bag onto the ground in front of the serpent. The serpent was hungry, so he could not resist stopping to eat the bone. When the bone was eaten, the serpent again began to come toward the ladder, but Kwaku Tsin merely tossed another bone, so the serpent had to stop to eat it. Kwaku Tsin kept doing this until all the people had reached the heavens and all the bones were gone.

Then Kwaku Tsin began to climb up himself, the serpent in hot pursuit. However, every time the serpent got too close, Kwaku Tsin began playing the fiddle. He played so well and joyfully that the serpent had to go back down the ladder and dance. Kwaku Tsin kept going in this wise until he reached the heavens, the serpent hard on his heels. Just as the serpent was about to catch him in its jaws, Kwaku Tsin took out his knife and cut the ladder away, sending the serpent crashing to his death far below.

As a reward for his bravery and cleverness, the gods turned Kwaku Tsin into the sun and his father Anansi into the moon, and all the people Kwaku Tsin had rescued became the stars.

And so it is that Kwaku Tsin continues to help all his fellow people by providing them with light and warmth.

Part IV: Punishment and Reward

Kassa and the Heavy Feather
(*Mende, Sierra Leone*)

The Mende people live in Sierra Leone and parts of Liberia. This tale about a strong and boastful young man and a threatening bird of prey has a surprising twist ending.

Once there was a young man named Kassa Kena Ganina. He was tall and very, very strong. Kassa was fond of boasting that he was the strongest man in the whole world, and indeed his neighbors agreed that this must be true, for he was stronger than anyone else they knew.

Kassa had two friends named Iri Ba Farra and Kongo Li Ba Jelema. The three young men often went hunting together in the bush. Iri and Kongo hunted with bows, arrows, and spears; however, Kassa carried nothing but a long iron rod. One day, they went out hunting. Iri and Kongo had no luck. Every shot of the bow and throw of the spear went awry. But Kassa soon had killed twenty antelope with his iron rod, for as well as being strong, he was a swift runner.

Kassa piled up the antelope carcasses in a clearing.

He turned to his friends and said, "Iri, you stay here and make sure no animals steal the meat. Kongo and I are going to collect firewood."

"Very well," Iri replied, who watched as Kassa and Kongo went back into the trees on their errand.

All was quiet for some time, but suddenly, a giant Konoba bird flew down toward Iri and hovered above him. The Konoba bird was huge and had a long, curved beak and sharp talons.

The bird said, "Which one should I take? Should I take you, or should I take the meat?"

Iri took one look at the bird and was terrified.

"Take the meat!" he replied.

And so the bird swooped down and scooped up all twenty antelope in its talons and flew away.

Not long after the bird had left, Kassa and Kongo returned carrying loads of firewood.

"What happened to all the meat?" Kassa asked.

"A huge Konoba bird came and asked me whether it should take me or the meat," Iri replied. "I told it to take the meat."

"You should have told it to take yourself instead."

Another day, the three friends went into the bush to go hunting. Again, Kassa felled many antelope, which he piled in a clearing.

"This time, Iri will come with me for firewood, and Kongo will guard the meat," Kassa said.

And so he and Iri went back into the trees to get the wood while Kongo remained alone in the clearing.

It did not take long before the great Konobo bird swooped down toward Kongo.

"Which one should I take?" the bird asked. "Should I take you, or should I take the meat?"

"Take the meat!" Kongo shouted, quaking with fear.

And so the bird took up all the antelope in its talons and flew away.

When Iri and Kassa returned with the firewood, they saw that all the antelope were gone.

"Where did all the meat go?" Kassa asked.

"That bird came again," Kongo replied. "It was enormous and had great, sharp talons. It asked me if it should take me or the meat. I told it to take the meat!"

"You should have told it to take yourself. Next time we go hunting, I'll guard the meat, and the two of you will go and fetch the firewood."

The next time the three went hunting, Kassa stayed behind with the meat while the others went to get the firewood.

Again, the Konoba bird swooped down, and again it said, "Which one should I take? Should I take you, or should I take the meat?"

"You won't take either of us," Kassa replied, who struck the bird with his iron rod, hitting it and killing it instantly.

Now, when Kassa struck the bird, one of its feathers came loose and floated down onto Kassa's back. The feather was so heavy that Kassa fell to the ground and could not get back up again. Kassa lay there helpless until a woman carrying a child came down the path.

"Help me!" Kassa said. "I am stuck here! Go and find my friends Iri and Kongo, and ask them to come and help me. They're in the forest gathering firewood."

The woman went into the forest, found Iri and Kongo, and brought them back to where Kassa was still lying on the ground.

"What is the matter?" Iri asked.

"When I killed the Konoba bird, one of its feathers landed on my back," Kassa replied. "It's so heavy! I can't get up because of it!"

Iri tried to pick the feather off Kassa's back, but he couldn't lift it. Kongo and Iri then tried to pick the feather off Kassa's back, but it was too heavy even for two strong young men.

Now, the woman with the child had been standing and watching this the whole time. When Iri and Kongo stepped back to catch their breath, she went over to Kassa and blew on the feather, which floated away. Then she picked up the dead bird, handed it to her child to play with, and went on her way.

How Yams Came to the Ashanti
(*Ashanti, Ghana*)

The tale retold below is a legend created to explain important aspects of Ashanti culture. One of these aspects is the importance of yams to Ashanti cuisine. Yams play an important dietary role for the Ashanti and are used in ceremonies honoring ancestors, a practice central to Ashanti beliefs. The other aspect is the matrilineal organization of Ashanti society, which is divided into matrilineal clans and various lineages. One important type of lineage is the maximal lineage, which traces descent from a distant common female ancestor. The Ashanti word for maximal lineage is abusua, *supposedly derived from the name of the protagonist of this tale.*

Long ago, the Ashanti had difficulty growing enough food to feed themselves. They had many crops but could not produce enough to get them through the year. One day, a traveler came to an Ashanti village. The traveler was carrying a yam. A young man named Abu saw the traveler and was curious, for he had never seen a yam.

"What is that you are carrying?" Abu asked the traveler.

"This is a yam," the traveler replied.

"What is it for?"

"It is something to eat. You cook them, and then you eat them. They grow in the ground where I'm from."

Abu told the other people in his village about the yam.

"I'm going to see whether I can find some of these yams," he said. "Maybe if we planted those with our other crops, we'd have food all year round."

Abu made preparations for his journey, and when all was ready, he bade farewell to his family and friends and set out to find the country where the yams grew. He traveled through forests and across rivers. He walked across plains and over mountains. He traveled through many villages. Everywhere he went, he asked where the country was where the yams grew. Sometimes, the people gave him directions. Sometimes, they did not. It was a very long and tiring journey; however, finally, he arrived at the place where the yams grew.

Abu went to see the king of the place and said, "I come from a place where yams do not grow. I would like your permission to take some yams home, so my people can have food all year round."

The king replied, "I will give you my answer soon."

Then the king ordered his servants to take Abu to the guest house and see that he wanted for nothing.

A few days passed, and the king called Abu back into the audience chamber. "I have thought about your request, and I must deny it. Once your people have food all year round, they will become strong and may become my enemy. I cannot take that chance."

"That would not happen, Your Majesty," Abu replied. "We are but peaceful farmers. But now that we know where the yams grow, might we not try to take them by force to alleviate our hunger?"

"That is true. Here is what I propose. You send one of the sons of your village to be my hostage as surety that your people will not become my enemy. Then I will give you yams."

"Very well."

Abu set out on the long journey home.

When he arrived, he went to his father and said, "The king of the yam country says that he won't give us yams unless we send a son of our village to be a hostage. If you send one of your sons, we will have food to eat all year round."

"This I will not do," Abu's father replied. "I don't want my sons to have to go away from me."

Abu then went to his brother and made the same request. Abu's brother also refused. Abu asked all his other brothers, each of whom had many sons, and they all said no.

Abu returned to the yam country and told the king, "I asked my father and my brothers, but none of them would give one of their sons to be your hostage."

"That is too bad," the king replied. "I will not give your people any yams without the hostage coming to live with me."

Abu went back home feeling downtrodden. The hungry time was coming soon, and his people would have no yams to eat. He did not know who else to ask to send a hostage. Finally, he went to his sister. He had been reluctant to ask her because she had only one son, whereas his father and brothers each had many.

"Please send your son to be the hostage," Abu said. "Otherwise, our people will starve again."

"I will send him," Abu's sister replied. "Even though it breaks my heart to do so."

Abu and the boy went to the king of the yam country. The king welcomed the boy and made him part of the royal household. Then he gave Abu many yams to take home with him. The people planted the yams, and there was a fine crop at harvest time. The yams kept well for a long time, and so that year, for the first time, the people did not go hungry.

Abu thought for a long time about how his father and brothers would not help the people get yams to eat. Then he made a decision.

He called his father, brothers, and sister together and said, "None of you would give your sons to be the hostage so that we could have food all year round, except for my sister. She sent her only son while you had many sons. Therefore, when I die, my possessions will go to my nephew, who now lives with the king of the yam country, to honor him and his mother. I do this because it is by my nephew's sacrifice and my sister's that we now have food to eat all year round."

When Abu died, his cattle and property were brought to the yam country and given to his nephew. The Ashanti people thought that Abu had done a great deed by doing this, and so from then on, property was passed on not from father to son but from maternal uncles to their nephews.

You-are-wiser-than-the-king
(Hausa, Nigeria)

This Hausa tale rings the changes on many fairytale tropes, especially that of the wise commoner who outwits the foolish king. However, not content to do merely that, the tale then takes a turn into the magical and thence into the absurd, and in the process, also becomes a just-so story.

While it is not explicitly stated in the original story, presumably, the king has it in for You-are-wiser-than-the-king out of dudgeon over the presumptuous nature of the young man's name.

A long time ago, three slaves belonged to a king. The king had a son, and each of his three slaves had a son. The sons of the slaves were named He-who-will-not-see, The-gift-of-God, and You-are-wiser-than-the-king. When these sons were born, they were presented to the king, and when they had grown to adulthood, they also entered the king's service.

One day, the king gave a bundle of sorghum grain to He-who-will-not-see and another to The-gift-of-God, but to You-are-wiser-than-the-king, he gave only a bundle of husks. Then the king told the young men that they were each to return with three hundred bundles of sorghum the following year.

At harvest time, He-who-will-not-see and The-gift-of-God each brought three hundred bundles of grain to the king, but You-are-wiser-than-the-king brought three hundred bundles of husks from the grain that had been harvested.

"Where is the grain you were supposed to bring me?" the king asked the one who had brought the husks.

"I planted what you gave me," You-are-wiser-than-the-king replied. "And that's what grew."

"Very well."

Then the king gave a cow to He-who-will-not-see and another to The-gift-of-God, but to You-are-wiser-than-the-king, he gave a bull. He then told the young men that they were to bring him the calves that these cattle produced the following year.

A year went by, and at the appointed time, He-who-will-not-see and The-gift-of-God each brought the king two calves; however, You-are-wiser-than-the-king was absent because instead, he had taken an axe and climbed up into a dead tree behind the palace.

"You have brought your calves as ordered," the king said to the two young men. "But where is You-are-wiser-than-the-king?"

One of the courtiers replied, "We saw someone who looked like him up in that dead tree that stands behind your palace. He was chopping branches off the tree."

The king went to the tree, and just as the courtier had said, there was You-are-wiser-than-the-king, sitting in the tree and lopping off branches with his axe.

"What in the world are you doing up there?" the king asked.

"My father just had a baby, so I'm cutting firewood for him," You-are-wiser-than-the-king replied.

"Men can't have babies, and you know it. Stop being foolish."

"Oh, so you know that males can't have young, and yet you gave me a bull and then demanded that I bring you its calves?"

Since the king had no answer, he went back into his palace.

The king then gathered his advisors together and said, "What should I do about You-are-wiser-than-the-king? That lad is too clever by half, and I am afraid of him."

"Kill him," the advisors replied.

"How should I do this?"

"Dress You-are-wiser-than-the-king in the finest clothing. Give him a blue robe and turban, and trousers with blue stripes. Give him a fine horse, caparisoned, with a well-made saddle and bridle. Then dress your son in ragged slave's clothing, and put him on a scrawny nag with a bad saddle and bridle. Send them together on a journey and station gunmen in hiding along the road. Tell the gunmen to shoot the one wearing fine clothing and spare the one in ragged clothing. In this way, you will be rid of You-are-wiser-than-the-king."

The king did as his advisors told him, but You-are-wiser-than-the-king suspected something bad would happen because of his rich clothing. Therefore, he told one of his friends to hurry down the road carrying gourds full of beer and water and to wait there.

When You-are-wiser-than-the-king and the king's son came across the man with the gourds, You-are-wiser-than-the-king said to the king's son, "We have been traveling a long way under the hot sun. Let's have a drink."

So You-are-wiser-than-the-king bought the gourds full of water and beer from his friend. You-are-wiser-than-the-king gave the gourds full of beer to the king's son and kept the gourds full of water for himself. The two young men drank from one of their gourds, and soon the king's son felt quite tipsy.

A little way down the road, You-are-wiser-than-the-king said, "It's such a hot day, and I'm so thirsty. Let's drink again."

And so the king's son drank beer, and You-are-wiser-than-the-king drank water, and the king's son became tipsier.

They went on in this wise until the king's son was quite drunk.

"Dear, oh dear," You-are-wiser-than-the-king said to the king's son. "You can't go about in that fashion. Here, let's swap clothing and horses. That would be more fitting."

And because the king's son was so drunk, he didn't protest, and soon he was dressed in the blue robe, turban, and striped trousers and mounted on the fine horse, while You-are-wiser-than-the-king was wearing the ragged clothing and mounted on the scrawny nag.

They continued down the road until they came to where the king's gunmen were hidden. The gunmen took aim at the king's son, shot him, and he died. No sooner had the king's son's body hit the ground than You-are-wiser-than-the-king galloped back to the palace and shouted for the king to come out.

When the king came out, You-are-wiser-than-the-king said, "Who is my equal? Who is the equal of You-are-wiser-than-the-king?"

The king shouted, "I am!"

He then ran to pull You-are-wiser-than-the-king out of the saddle; however, You-are-wiser-than-the-king turned himself into a frog, and the king could not lay hold of him. So the king turned himself into a serpent and made to swallow the frog, but You-are-wiser-than-the-king turned himself into a mouse and scampered away. The king turned himself into a cat and nearly had the mouse in his claws when You-are-wiser-than-the-king turned himself into a red bird and flew away. The king then turned himself into a hawk, but the red bird flew into the eye of an old woman who was nearby, and there he became the pupil of her eye. The king then flew onto the face of the old woman and there became her eyebrow. That is why the pupil of the eye stays where it is, for fear that if it comes out, the eyebrow will catch him.

Maku Mawu and Maku Fia (*Unknown*)

This West African tale, which may come from Ghana, is another that partakes in the trope of the wise commoner who outwits a foolish king. However, unlike You-are-wiser-than-the-king, Maku Mawu's rise to good fortune and escape from death is due largely to luck rather than his own cleverness.

Maku Mawu and Maku Fia were two men who were great friends. Maku Mawu's name meant "I will die God's death," and Maku Fia's meant "I will die the king's death." Now, these were not the names given to them at their birth; they were nicknames they had for one another, but since everyone always heard the two friends call one another by those names, everyone else used them, too.

One day, the king heard about the two friends and their unusual names. He sent for them, thinking to ask them why they had taken these names. The king was especially curious about Maku Mawu since he thought it offensive that someone would take that name in the first place. However, Maku Fia's name did not bother the king; in fact, he thought it was rather a good name. The king spoke to the two men for a while and then invited them to come back to a feast he was holding in three days' time. As parting gifts, he gave Maku Mawu a large yam, while to Maku Fia, he gave a large, round stone.

On the way home, Maku Fia said, "You are lucky, my friend. The king gave you a yam. At least you can eat that for dinner. All he gave me was this stone. It's very heavy, and what am I going to do with a stone, anyway?"

"I'll trade you the yam for the stone," Maku Mawu replied. "I have more yams at home."

And so Maku Fia handed over the stone and took the yam in exchange.

When Maku Mawu got home, he examined the stone closely. He thought it sounded a bit hollow, so he broke it in half. Inside the stone was a pile of ornaments made of gold and other fine things.

Oho! Maku Mawu thought. *I can't wait to see the king's face when I show up to the feast wearing all of this.*

Then Maku Mawu hid the finery so that no one else would know about it.

On the day of the feast, Maku Mawu put on his best clothing and all the jewelry that had been inside the stone. Maku Fia went to the feast wearing his best clothing but no jewelry, for he had none. When the two men presented themselves to the king at the feast, the king seethed inside to see the wrong man wearing the finery he had intended to go to Maku Fia.

"Maku Fia," the king said. "What did you do with that stone I gave you?"

"Oh, that? It was awfully heavy, so I traded it for the yam you gave my friend here."

Since the king had not told them they could not trade their gifts, he had no excuse to punish Maku Mawu. Throughout the feast, the king thought of nothing but how he could trick Maku Mawu and so have an excuse to punish or even kill him. Then the king had an idea. At the end of the feast, he presented Maku Mawu with a ring from his own finger.

"This is a very fine ring, and it is important that you not lose it," the king said. "In fact, I would like you to come back here with the ring in seven days to show me that you are keeping it properly. If you lose the ring, you lose your life. Do you understand?"

Maku Mawu said that he understood and began to see that the king was not being generous. No, the king was trying to set him up in some way, so when Maku Mawu got home, he dug a little hole in the wall of his house, put the ring inside, and then filled the hole in again so that no one but himself would know where the ring was.

On the second day after the feast, the king summoned Maku Mawu's wife to speak to him.

"Your husband took one of my rings by mistake yesterday, and now I would like it back," the king said. "Can you get it and bring it to me?"

"Yes, certainly, sir," Maku Mawu's wife replied.

"Mind you, don't tell him. This needs to be our little secret."

Maku Mawu's wife agreed not to say anything to her husband. She went home and looked for the ring, but couldn't find it anywhere. She looked all that day and all the next and still couldn't find the ring.

At the end of the second day, she said to Maku Mawu, "Husband, what happened to the ring the king gave you?"

Not thinking ill of his wife, who did not know her husband's life would be forfeit if the ring went missing, Maku Mawu replied, "Oh, I dug a little hole in the wall over there and put the ring inside. I wanted to keep it safe for the king."

The next day, while Maku Mawu was out working on their farm, the wife searched the wall until she found where the ring was hidden. She dug the ring out of the wall and brought it to the king, who paid her a good reward for her help.

On the sixth day after the feast, the king sent a messenger reminding Maku Mawu that he needed to present himself in court the next day, bearing the king's ring. Maku Mawu then went to dig the ring out of its hiding place but found it was gone. He asked his wife and all his neighbors whether they had seen the ring, but they all said they had not.

Well, that's the end of me, Maku Mawu thought. *I really shouldn't have teased the king with that jewelry.*

Meanwhile, the king had been wearing the ring and thinking about how he was going to execute Maku Mawu. On the evening before Maku Mawu was to come to the court, the king took off the ring and put it on a dish. The next morning, the king sent messengers summoning the people to the meeting place to see a man get his just punishment for disobeying the king's orders, and he also told his servants to take all the dishes in his house and clean them. When the servants took the dishes to the nearby river to wash them, they paid no attention to what was on the dishes, so the ring fell into the water.

The time for Maku Mawu's punishment neared, so the king went to find the ring to put on his finger, but it was nowhere to be found.

Oh, well, the king thought. *I don't need the ring to finish the day's business anyway.*

At the assembly place, the king called Maku Mawu forward and demanded his ring back.

"I'm afraid I don't have it, Your Majesty," Maku Mawu said. "I don't know what happened to it. I am prepared to pay the penalty for losing the ring, but may I have some time to get my affairs in order before I die?"

"You have four hours," the king replied. "At the end of that time, you must come back here, where you will be beheaded for your insolence."

Maku Mawu went home and put his affairs in order. When that was done, he still had some time left, and he was hungry. He went to the river and caught a fish to eat as his last meal. He cut the fish open to gut it, and what should pop out but the king's ring! Maku Mawu shouted for joy and ran back to the king's compound, holding the ring up high.

"I found the ring! I found the ring! Your Majesty, look! Here is your ring back!" he shouted.

The king agreed that Maku Mawu had kept his side of the bargain and pardoned him.

The people, for their part, marveled at how well Maku Mawu's name fitted him, for surely here was a man who would only die when God said it was his time and not by the king's command.

Ohia and the Language of the Animals
(*Akan, Ghana*)

This story centers partly around the collection of palm tree sap, a common practice throughout West Africa and many other parts of the world where palm trees grow. In Africa, sometimes the entire tree is chopped down and the sap collected from the stump; however, at other times, a tapper is affixed to the tree, which is left standing. Palm tree sap begins to ferment almost immediately upon contact with the air, yielding a sweet, cloudy-white, mildly alcoholic beverage that is both a standard drink and used at weddings and other important ceremonies and rituals.

Once there was a man named Ohia who had a wife named Ariwehu. Ohia and Ariwehu were very unlucky people. If Ohia sowed a field of sorghum, the birds would come and eat all the seed. If Ariwehu tried to weave a piece of cloth, her loom would break. If the couple planted yams in their garden, something would happen to make the tubers rot and be unfit to eat. It did not take long before Ohia and Ariwehu had next to nothing to eat and wear.

One evening, Ohia and Ariwehu sat outside their house at sunset, their stomachs grumbling because they had had so little to eat that day.

"What will we do, husband?" Ariwehu asked. "If we don't find a way to get money soon, we will starve, and we will also be naked when we die because our clothes are falling apart."

"Don't worry," Ohia replied. "I will go to that rich farmer who lives down the way and offer to clear some land for him. There are palm trees there, so when I chop down the trees, I will collect the sap to make palm wine. We can sell the wine at the market, which will turn our fortunes around, even after giving the farmer his portion of the sale."

Ariwehu agreed that this was a good plan, so in the morning, Ohia went to the farmer and offered to clear land, sell the palm sap, and share the proceeds from the sale.

The farmer agreed to this plan, saying, "Here, take these pots. I expect you don't have any of your own, and I don't want to lose out on the palm wine sale."

Ohia and his wife chopped down several palm trees and set the pots beneath them to catch the sap. They went home that evening very tired and still hungry but hopeful that things would now start to get better for them both. However, when they went to collect the pots in the morning, they found that every single one had been smashed, and all the palm sap was gone.

Not wanting to say anything to the farmer about this, Ohia and Ariwehu borrowed pots from some friends and set them out to collect sap. But that night, the same thing happened, so the poor couple was forced to go to the farmer and explain the loss of the pots and the sap.

"It's not your fault that a thief and vandal came to my field," the farmer said. "Here, have some more pots, as many as you need."

This time, Ohia decided to lay in wait to catch the thief instead of going home after setting out the pots,.

"He'll not get away with it this time," Ohia said to his wife. "Not if I have to chase him all the way to the ends of the earth."

Ohia hid in some bushes near where the pots had been set out and waited. Midnight came and went, with no sign of the thief. Another hour passed, and then another. And then Ohia heard it: The unmistakable sound of a pot being shattered. Ohia followed the sound, moving as stealthily as he could. There, he found a deer pouring the sap from one of Ohia's pots into a large pot of its own. Apparently, the deer had already stolen the sap from one pot and had broken it before moving on to this one. Ohia lunged at the deer, thinking to catch it, but it spotted Ohia just in time. The deer dropped its pot on the ground and fled, Ohia in hot pursuit.

On and on, the deer ran, but Ohia did not give up. Ohia was hungry and thirsty, but his anger gave him strength as they ran through the trees and across streams. They ran through the rest of the night. They ran as day broke and the sun rose in the sky. Finally, at midday, the deer came to a hill and ran up it. Ohia ran up in pursuit, and when he reached the top of the hill, he found himself in a gathering of animals. On a stool at one end of the ring of animals sat a leopard, who clearly was the king.

"Your Majesty! This man followed me here! Mete out justice to him!" the deer said.

"It is death for men to come to the council of the animals," the leopard replied. "But maybe you have a reason for being here. I will wait until I hear your story before deciding your fate."

"Your Majesty," Ohia said. "I am but a poor man. All of my crops have failed, so my wife and I have nothing to eat. My wife's loom broke, and we have no money to buy another, so all our clothes are in tatters. So, I hired myself out to a rich farmer to clear his land and collect palm sap for making palm wine, which I hoped to sell for a little money for food and clothing. I chopped down the trees and set out my pots to catch the sap, but in the morning, I found the sap gone and all the pots broken. I had to borrow more pots to catch the sap because I am too poor to buy them. The following night, the sap disappeared, and the pots were broken. On the third night, I determined to catch the thief, and that's when I saw this deer taking the sap and breaking the pots the rich farmer had kindly lent me. When I tried to catch the deer, he ran, so I chased him here. I did not know that this was where he was leading me. I apologize for interrupting your council."

The leopard consulted with his advisors about what should be done.

When the leopard was satisfied that he had a just answer, he said, "Man, we hold you blameless in this. You have done nothing wrong. The deer, however, will be punished because I had given him money to go and buy palm wine, not steal wine that did not belong to him. I apologize for his actions, which have caused you and your wife great distress. I can't give you back the broken pots or the missing wine, but I can give you one thing—the ability to understand the language of the animals. That is your recompense for your losses, but it comes on condition that you never tell anyone that you have this gift, on pain of death."

Ohia bowed and thanked the leopard king for his generosity, promising to never tell anyone about the gift or what had happened on the hilltop that day.

When Ohia got home, his wife asked, "Where have you been? Did you catch the thief?"

"No," Ohia replied. "He ran away. I chased him, but he was too swift for me. It was a long chase, and it took me a long time to return home. Come, let's go set our pots out again. Now that the thief knows we're on to him, maybe he'll leave us alone."

Ohia and his wife set to finishing the work of clearing the land and setting out the pots. In the morning, the pots were full of sap, and Ohia got a good price for it at the market. After giving the farmer his share, Ohia and Ariwehu still had plenty left over. From that day forward, Ohia and Ariwehu's fortunes improved. Their crops grew well, and they had full harvests. Ariwehu made fine cloth on her new loom. They had a little son of whom they were very proud. Life was good at last.

One day, Ohia went to bathe in a pond near his house. While in the water, he heard one of his hens talking to her chicks as they foraged for insects at the edge of the garden.

"Now, children," the hen said. "We only ever scratch for insects and other good things away from the house because there are three pots full of gold buried in the back garden. If we scratch too much, the pots will be unburied, and we mustn't let the people know about it."

Ohia pretended not to understand what the hen had said; however, when she and her brood had moved elsewhere to do their scratching, Ohia took a spade and dug in the place the hen had told her chicks about. Just as the hen had said, there were three large pots full of gold. Ohia brought them into his house, telling Ariwehu that he had come across them accidentally while working in the garden and saying nothing about the hen's instruction to her children. If life had been good for Ohia and Ariwehu before, now it was even better, for the gold in the pots was enough for them to live comfortably for the rest of their lives.

Now that Ohia was rich, he decided to take another wife. The woman he chose was lame and had a bad disposition. She was the opposite of Ariwehu, who was always kind and courteous to everyone. This new wife also suspected everyone of laughing at her disability. She especially suspected Ohia and Ariwehu of laughing at her behind her back and often accused them of this, which they firmly denied because it was untrue. When the woman eavesdropped on conversations between Ohia and Ariwehu, she never heard a bad word spoken about herself, but this did nothing to convince her that Ohia and Ariwehu respected her.

One night, as Ohia and Ariwehu lay together in bed, Ohia overheard some mice talking.

"Shh!" one of the mice said. "You'll wake him up!"

"I can't wake him up if he's not asleep yet, stupid," the other mouse replied.

"Fine. You keep an eye on him, then, and when he's asleep, we'll go and raid the pantry."

"Fine."

Ohia thought this little conversation very amusing and laughed out loud.

No sooner had he done so than his second wife rushed into the room. "There! I caught you! You two were laughing at me, just like you always do!"

"What are you talking about?" Ohia asked.

"Just now, you were laughing. You were laughing about me. I know it!" the second wife.

"I was doing no such thing."

"We weren't talking about you at all," Ariwehu said. "I don't even know what he was laughing at."

"You're lying," the second wife replied.

"We are not," Ohia and Ariwehu said.

"Prove it then."

However, Ohia could not reveal what he was laughing about without revealing his secret and thus losing his life, so he held his peace.

"Well, if that's how it's going to be, I'll take this to the chief," the second wife said. "He'll make you talk."

And so, in the morning, the second wife went to the chief and explained what had happened.

The chief summoned Ohia and said, "Come now, tell us what you were laughing at, and put this thing to rest."

"I'm sorry, O chief, but I cannot tell you," Ohia replied.

The chief knew that Ohia was an honest man and so sent him home, but the second wife continued to pester the chief until finally, he told Ohia that he would be held to account before the village council. Ohia knew that he would have no choice but to obey, so he set his affairs in order, distributing all his wealth to Ariwehu, their children, and his servants.

On the day of the village council, the chief told Ohia to stand forth and explain himself. Ohia told the story of how he and Ariwehu were living in poverty and tried to collect palm sap to sell so that they could have food and clothing. He told how he chased the deer up the hill to the animals' council, how the leopard king gave him the ability to understand the speech of the animals, and how he would die if he told anyone about it.

"I was laughing because I was listening to two little mice talking about raiding my pantry," Ohia said. "It was very sweet and made me laugh. It had nothing to do with my second wife."

No sooner had Ohia said this than he dropped dead as a stone.

The village then realized that Ohia, whom everyone knew as a good and honest man, had been treated unjustly by his second wife, who was seized and burned as a witch. Her ashes were then scattered to the four winds, which is how jealousy and selfishness increased throughout the whole world, whereas before that, people had been more kind and generous.

The Cow-Tail Switch (*Jabo, Liberia*)

In many African cultures, switches or fly-whisks made of cattle tails are important symbols of authority. They are often carried by kings, chiefs, shamans, and other important persons. The long hair at the end of the whisk hangs loose, while the shaft is often decorated with patterns made of beads. Sometimes, the end of the shaft is made of wood carved into a human or another figure. The story about a cow-tail switch retold below is a version of one originally collected by anthropologist George Herzog in Liberia.

Once there was a hunter named Ogaloussa. He had a wife and many fine sons. One day, Ogaloussa took his weapons and went into the forest to hunt, but he never returned. Ogaloussa's children often wondered what had become of their father. They told each other stories of their memories of him. However, as time passed, the children thought of their father and spoke of him less and less until finally, they thought and spoke of him not at all.

Now, Ogaloussa's wife was with child on that fateful day when her husband did not return. Many months passed after Ogaloussa's disappearance, and finally, the child was born. The baby was a boy, and his mother named him Puli. Puli grew and learned to walk and talk.

One day, when he was still quite small, he looked at his older brothers and asked, "Where is my father?"

The brothers all looked at each other. They had not thought about their father or spoken of him for a long time.

"Yes, where is he?" they asked one another. "Let's go and look for him."

And so the older boys set out to find their father. They found his trail, and after much looking, they came across a pile of bones. Next to the bones were hunting weapons they recognized as belonging to their father. While hunting, something must have happened to Ogaloussa, and he died there in the bush.

One of the sons said, "I know how a skeleton can be put back together," and he began to rearrange his father's bones.

When all the bones were properly placed, another son said, "I can put muscle and flesh and skin on the bones."

Soon, the bones were covered by flesh and skin, and the boys saw that it was indeed their father lying there.

A third son said, "I will put blood back into the body."

And so the heart began to beat, and blood began to course through the veins.

The fourth son said, "I can give him breath and movement."

Suddenly, the body took a great shuddering breath, and Ogaloussa, restored to life, sat up and looked around him.

"Where are my weapons?" he asked.

"They are old and rusted now," one of his sons replied. "But they are yours, so we return them to you."

When Ogaloussa had taken back his weapons, he returned home with his sons. Ogaloussa's wife was overjoyed to see her husband again. Ogaloussa was also glad to be home, but he was not ready to go out into the village yet. He stayed home for four days, and on the fifth day, he had a cow slaughtered so that he could give a great feast for his village to celebrate his return from the dead.

Ogaloussa took the cow's tail and made a switch out of it. He decorated the handle of the switch with many beads and ribbons. Ogaloussa brought it with him to the feast. It was the most beautiful switch anyone had ever seen. Soon, people were asking Ogaloussa whether they could have the switch; however, Ogaloussa would not give it to them. Ogaloussa realized that he would need to speak to all the people about the switch, or they would keep asking him for it.

Ogaloussa stood up to speak, and everyone stopped what they were doing and listened.

Ogaloussa said, "One day, I went hunting and was attacked by a leopard. I died. But then my sons came and found me and brought me back to life. Each of them played a part in restoring me. The one who did the most to bring me back to my family and village shall have this switch."

Immediately one of the sons shouted, "I gave him back his bones! The switch should come to me!"

"No, it should be mine!" another shouted. "I put the flesh back on the bones!"

"Flesh and bones aren't much good without blood in the veins," the third said. "Give the switch to me!"

"Father never would have come home without breath and movement," the fourth said. "I should get the switch."

Now, the people who had listened to Ogaloussa's speech and the replies of his sons began to argue about which son most deserved to have the switch. Some agreed that the one who had arranged the bones should have it. Others thought that the one who restored Ogaloussa's flesh was most deserving. On and on, the people argued. On and on, the sons argued.

Finally, Ogaloussa said, "I have made my decision."

Then he went to little Puli and handed the switch to him, saying, "I am giving the switch to Puli, for if he had not asked where I was, I never would have been found, and if I never had been found, I never would have been restored to life. Puli is the one who did the most to bring me back home."

And all of the villagers and Ogaloussa's sons agreed this was correct. Puli was the one who deserved to have the switch.

Here's another book by Matt Clayton that you might like

Free Bonus from Captivating History (Available for a Limited time)

Hi History Lovers!

Now you have a chance to join our exclusive history list so you can get your first history ebook for free as well as discounts and a potential to get more history books for free! Simply visit the link below to join.

Captivatinghistory.com/ebook

Also, make sure to follow us on Facebook, Twitter and Youtube by searching for Captivating History.

www.ingramcontent.com/pod-product-compliance
Lightning Source LLC
Chambersburg PA
CBHW061700130726
47996CB00006B/2105